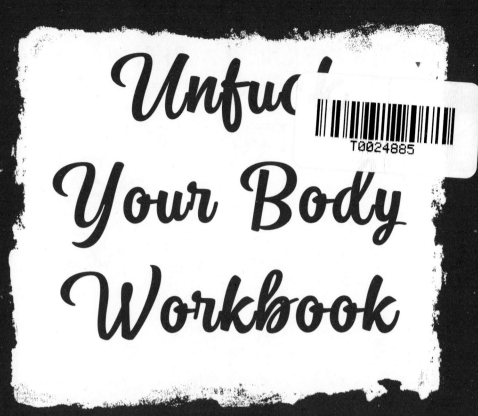

# Unfuck Your Body Workbook

## USING SCIENCE TO EAT, SLEEP, BREATHE, MOVE, AND FEEL BETTER

Faith G. Harper,
PhD, LPC-S, ACS, ACN

Microcosm Publishing
Portland, OR

# UNFUCK YOUR BODY WORKBOOK

**Using Science to Eat, Sleep, Breathe, Move, and Feel Better**

Part of the 5 Minute Therapy Series

© Faith G. Harper, PhD, LPC-S, ACS, ACN

This edition © Microcosm Publishing, 2021

First edition, first published July 27th, 2021

ISBN 9781621061755

This is Microcosm #554

Cover and design by Joe Biel

Edited by Elly Blue

For a catalog, write or visit:

Microcosm Publishing

2752 N Williams Ave.

Portland, OR 97227

503-799-2698

www.Microcosm.Pub

These worksheets can be used on their own, or as a companion to **Unfuck Your Body** by Dr. Faith G. Harper.

***To join the ranks of high-class stores that feature Microcosm titles, talk to your rep:*** In the U.S. **Como** (Atlantic), **Fujii** (Midwest), **Book Travelers West** (Pacific), **Turnaround** in Europe, **Manda/UTP** in Canada, **New South** in Australia, and **GPS** in Asia, India, Africa, and South America. Sold in the gift market by **Faire.**

Did you know that you can buy our books directly from us at sliding scale rates? Support a small, independent publisher and pay less than Amazon's price at www.Microcosm.Pub

Global labor conditions are bad, and our roots in industrial Cleveland in the 70s and 80s made us appreciate the need to treat workers right. Therefore, our books are MADE IN THE USA.

# MICROCOSM·PUBLISHING

Microcosm Publishing is Portland's most diversified publishing house and distributor with a focus on the colorful, authentic, and empowering. Our books and zines have put your power in your hands since 1996, equipping readers to make positive changes in their lives and in the world around them. Microcosm emphasizes skill-building, showing hidden histories, and fostering creativity through challenging conventional publishing wisdom with books and bookettes about DIY skills, food, bicycling, gender, self-care, and social justice. What was once a distro and record label was started by Joe Biel in his bedroom and has become among the oldest independent publishing houses in Portland, OR. We are a politically moderate, centrist publisher in a world that has inched to the right for the past 80 years.

# TABLE OF CONTENTS

# INTRODUCTION

**W**here do we even start with talking about how bodies get fucked up?

We get sick or injured. Trauma takes root, directly affecting our physical body as much as our brain. Stress seizes us up. Our toxic environments and food systems poison us. We experience pain. Our immune systems freak out and we don't know why. We have kids, or don't. We get busy and stop exercising. Years of insomnia catch up with us. We have surgery or take medication that changes our bodies. Or, most common of all, our personal meat puppet gets older and less tolerant of our bullshit.

We can't talk about bodies without talking about our brains, and vice versa—because our bodies and minds influence each other in every area of our physical and emotional lives. Your emotional and mental health do not exist outside of the body you live in. So this workbook is designed to help you better work with your mind-body connection to support your wellness.

The accompanying book, Unfuck Your Body, is about how the body and mind communicate with each other using the vagus nerve, and the enormous role trauma, inflammation, toxicity, and stress plays in that communication and our overall health. And most of all, it's about how we can feel better, by improving our body-brain awareness, developing habits that support the brain and body, and accessing treatments that serve our physical and mental health.

While my books and workbooks are designed to compliment each other, they are also designed to function on their own. Because nothing upsets my budget-loving heart like finding out I bought one thing, but have to buy another to make it work. Like, what do you even *mean,* the cord is sold separately?

So everything that needs explaining gets explained. And if you didn't read the book and kinda think, "Ah, that's kinda interesting," you can totally go get it and do a deeper dive on the research. But this is about connecting dots in your own life, so you can make whatever changes are in your power to make, increasing your ability to be as healthy as you possibly can even if everything around you is fundamentally broken and everyone around you is a total assclown. We can't fix the system if we aren't taking care of ourselves as best we can within it.

Okay, before we dig in: There will be no calorie counting. Either consumed in food or burned during exercise. There will be no guilting or shaming. There is zero information in here about changing the shape or size of who you are in any way. This is *all* about reconnecting to yourself.

Nothing in here is telling you to be fundamentally different than who you are. Your body contains *you* therefore it is a glorious creature that I am glad is alive on the planet. But I am also aware that sometimes we have taken such an emotional beating over topics like food and movement that even the gentlest approach may feel pretty barbed. So you have my full and enthusiastic permission to skip anything that is too much right now. If the point is to best care for yourself, start with topics that don't make you want to hide in a closet. You can always go back to those sections later, nothing was printed with disappearing ink.

And lastly? I need to make the "This is not medical advice" disclaimer. I'm a doctor, but not the MD kind. And while I am a licensed clinician (as well as certified in clinical nutrition, breathwork, meditation, yoga, and everything else I talk about here) I am not on *your* treatment team. So doing all this work will go way better with your actual treatment team. Your PCP, therapist, pain specialist, meditation instructor, etc. And please tell them I *did* say I'm not trying to override any of their treatment recommendations, but I do write with a holistic approach in mind, supporting everything they are providing to help you. Same team. We got this.

# SUDs

Let's start with a metric. I'm pretty sure no one leaves therapy school without the SUDs in their back pocket. SUDs stands for Subjective Units of Distress, and is a scale (usually 0-10 or 0-100 if you wanna get sassy with it) used to measure your intensity of distress. Only you know your insides, and SUDs is the best way (no matter how imperfect) to make that experience known. You're right, it's not an objective measurement like your pulse or vagal tone. Because we aren't focusing on that, we are focusing on how you feel and how it's affecting your ability to do important life shit.

We're going to use SUDs in a bunch of the exercises throughout this book, so go ahead and make notes here about what each level looks and feels like in your experience.

0 = Totally fine. Peaceful and settled in your body, no underlying agitation, upsetness, anxiety, or stress.

1 = Basically okay. Not upset, maybe if you were being super aware you might notice something feels a little unpleasant but it's not a big deal.

2 = A little upset. Maybe not even noticeable if you were busy, but if you're paying attention you would recognize something is bothering you a little.

3 = A little worried, noticing that you're mildly upset.

4 = Upset enough that it isn't easy to ignore. You can handle it, but it definitely doesn't feel good.

5 = Definitely uncomfortable, sorta upset. It feels unpleasant but it's still manageable with effort.

6 = Feeling bad. Recognizing you definitely need to do something about this.

7 = Heading into freak out. Sorta still in control, but almost barely.

8 = This is the official freak out point. No good is coming from this.

9 = Feeling at the edge. Oftentimes a 9 feels a lot like a 10 because you are getting really desperate. You're not at the point of unbearable quite yet, but are very scared that you are losing control and of what may happen.

10 = The worst it has ever felt or could feel. It feels literally unbearable and you feel out of control of your whole personhood.

# RELAXATION, SOOTHING, AND GROUNDING TECHNIQUES

**W**e're going to start this workbook with a whole bunch of ways you can relax your body and reconnect your body and mind *right now*. We're going to get into some harder stuff later, so let's give you the tools you need to deal with that and anything else that comes up in your life.

The problem with doing more intense emotional work is that we have to have a measure of control over ourselves. Meaning, we need skills to do the heavy shit without losing ourselves in the pain over and over again.

And these are the skills. Relaxation and self-soothing and all that other jazz are just ways of self-regulating when we're feeling over activated.

## Self-Soothing Tool Kit

In Dialectical Behavioral Therapy, creating an actual, physical toolkit for self-soothing is a common therapeutic intervention. The idea is that you use different items to connect to all five of your senses (or however many you want)  to reground you in your body and the present moment. These are tools to connect back to your window of tolerance by signaling safety to your vagal system. My office is full of such items and this is something you can create for yourself to access at home. Or make a portable one—or a collection of images or sounds on your phone—to use any time.

## VISION

○ Photos of people you love

○ Photos of places that are soothing to you

○ Images of artwork you love

○ Images with affirmations/quotes

○ A glitter bottle (instructions for making one below!)

○

○

○

○

## TOUCH

○ Clay, putty, play-doh

○ Fidget toys (like spinners or fidget rings)

○ Pom-poms or puffs

○ Stress ball or squeeze ball

○ Feather

○ Tactile blanket (or small square of tactile fabric for portability)

○ Lotion or body oil for self-massage

○ Weighted blanket (full-body or lap-sized)

○ Microwavable heat wrap (even if you don't warm it up, it adds weight)

○ Tactile socks, mittens, and other clothing

○

○

○

○

## TASTE

○ Gum

○ Hard candies

○ Individual bags of tea, hot chocolate, etc.

○ Mints

○ Throat spray

○ Crunchy chips or pretzels in individual servings

○

○

○

○

## SOUND

○ White noise machine

○ Soothing nature sounds (apps, downloads, YouTube videos)

○ Playlist of favorite music

○ Mini chimes, meditation bowl, chant recordings

○

○

○

○

## SMELL

- ◯ Essential oils
- ◯ Fragrant teas
- ◯ Coffee beans
- ◯ Loose tobacco
- ◯ Dried flowers or herbs
- ◯ Incense
- ◯ Scented candles
- ◯ Room sprays
- ◯ Perfumes
- ◯
- ◯
- ◯
- ◯

## PERSONAL TOOLKIT PLAN

| Vision | Touch | Taste | Sound | Smell |
|--------|-------|-------|-------|-------|
|        |       |       |       |       |

# Glitter Bottles

These glitter bottles are meant to be soothing and something to anchor on while your nervous system calms down. They are super cheap to make and can last forever. We have a few of them in the waiting room of my office that I made years ago. My work wife sees some kids in her practice who are quite adept at breaking stuff, but the bottles live on. Flip them over or shake them up and watch the glitter resettle while your body resettles.

You will need:

- Clear plastic bottles (ones that came with a drink inside are perfect, like water or gatorade)

- Water (from the tap is totally fine)

- Food coloring or dye

- Glitter or confetti

- Oil (any oil is fine but I recommend baby oil or clear mineral oil, so you won't have a yellowish tint)

- Glue (do not skip this part!)

Fill the bottles halfway up with water and add a few drops of food coloring or dye. Add your glitter or confetti then top off the bottle with oil. Dollop glue in the lid before screwing it back on and let it dry completely before you use it. It will never open again unless you yeet it against a wall, so you don't have to worry about an accidental mess.


# Lotion Playdough

This doesn't last as long as the water bottles do, but I've also made this for my office. I like this particular recipe because I have a lotion-buying problem. I own (and continue to buy) far more lotion that my skin can absorb in my lifetime, so this is a fun way to use it up. All you need to do is add ½ cup of lotion and 1 cup of cornstarch into a bowl. If the lotion is unscented you can add essential oils easily, if it's lightly scented you can still add some to enhance the smell. Mix it all together and that's it. You can portion it off into smaller amounts and use a little at a time. It's astonishing how grubby all playdough gets, whether store bought or homemade, and I've found it usually is growing fur before it even gets a chance to dry out.

## DIY Stress Ball

I was obsessed with these as a kid and had no idea they were so easy to make. You want to start with a balloon. Blow it up and release the air to stretch it out some. This will make it easier to add a funnel to the neck of it to add stuff inside. You can fill it with cornstarch, flour, uncooked rice, whatever you've got on hand. Remove the funnel and work any extra air out of the balloon before knotting it closed.

## Weighted Neck Wrap or Lap Blanket

Weighted blankets are now entering the domain of the affordable. I've had one in my office for years and it was hundreds of dollars and purchased online. And now you can find them for $29.99 at Target (and the weighted stuffies in the kid's section are under $20).

I love the availability but know that can still be more money than we have to spend. Back when they were hundreds, I figured out ways to make smaller ones without sewing because I am not allowed around sewing machines.

For the easiest neck wrap, use a long sock and fill it with uncooked rice (or buckwheat hulls if you wanna be fancy) and knot off the end. Bonus is that these can be warmed in the microwave or put in the freezer if you would like temperature sensation changes as well as the weight.

For a heavier lapblanket, the same idea applies. I filled two gallon ziploc bags (the freezer grade ones tend to be a little sturdier) with uncooked rice (just fill the bag, no specific amount) then covered each bag with a second bag for extra security and stability. I taped the two together with duct tape and slid the whole thing into a pillow case which zipped closed. This one shouldn't go in the microwave, but it is the perfect amount of lap or foot weight for grounding.

# Progressive Muscle Relaxation

The purpose of this exercise is to gain awareness of how our body is operating from the inside. You know, that interoception thing I was yammering on about. Actively engaging in progressive muscle relaxation exercises effectively loosens and relaxes the muscles. By tightening a muscle and then releasing, you can feel the difference between tense and relaxed.

Make sure not to do any movements that cause pain. If any of these exercises cause discomfort, ease up or stop. Sometimes if you are very tense already, actively tensing your muscles with progressive muscle relaxation exercise will not be helpful. If this is the case, you may want to try passive progressive muscle relaxation exercises instead, meaning you just focus on relaxing parts of your body, rather than tensing and then relaxing to feel the difference.

Here is a script for the guided progressive muscle relaxation exercise. You can read it as you go or have someone read it to you:

• Find a comfortable position sitting, standing, or lying down. You can change positions any time during the exercise.

• Breathe in forcefully and deeply, and hold this breath.

• Hold it...hold it... and now release. Let all the air go out slowly, and release all the tension.

• Take another deep breath in. Hold it.... and then exhale slowly, allowing the tension to leave your body with the air.

• Now breathe even more slowly and gently... breathe in....hold....out... ...breathe in...hold...out…

• Continue to breathe slowly and gently. Allow your breathing to relax you.

- Focus on the large muscles of your legs. Tighten all your leg muscles. Now tense them even further. Hold onto this tension. Feel how tight and tense the muscles in your legs are right now. Squeeze the muscles harder, tighter...

- Continue to hold this tension. Feel the muscles wanting to give up this tension. Hold it for a few moments more.... and now relax. Let all the tension go. Feel the muscles in your legs going limp, loose, and relaxed. Notice how relaxed the muscles feel now. Feel the difference between tension and relaxation. Enjoy the pleasant feeling of relaxation in your legs.

- Now focus on the muscles in your arms. Tighten your shoulders, upper arms, lower arms, and hands. Squeeze your hands into tight fists. Tense the muscles in your arms and hands as tightly as you can.

- Squeeze harder.... harder..... hold the tension in your arms, shoulders, and hands. Feel the tension in these muscles. Hold it for a few moments more.... and now release.

- Let the muscles of your shoulders, arms, and hands relax and go limp. Feel the relaxation as your shoulders lower into a comfortable position and your hands relax at your sides. Allow the muscles in your arms to relax completely.

- Focus again on your breathing. Slow, even, regular breaths. Breathe in relaxation.... and breathe out tension..... in relaxation....and out tension....

- Continue to breathe slowly and rhythmically.

- Now focus on the muscles of your buttocks. Tighten these muscles as much as you can.

- Hold this tension..... and then release.

- Relax your muscles.

• Tighten the muscles of your back now. Feel your back tightening, pulling your shoulders back and tensing the muscles along your spine. Arch your back slightly as you tighten these muscles. Hold.... and relax.

• Let all the tension go. Feel your back comfortably relaxing into a good and healthy posture.

• Turn your attention now to the muscles of your chest and stomach. Tighten and tense these muscles. Tighten them further...hold this tension.... and release.

• Relax the muscles of your trunk.

• Finally, tighten the muscles of your face. Scrunch your eyes shut tightly, wrinkle your nose, and tighten your cheeks and chin. Hold this tension in your face.... and relax.

• Release all the tension. Feel how relaxed your face is.

• Notice all of the muscles in your body.... notice how relaxed your muscles feel. Allow any last bits of tension to drain away. Enjoy the relaxation you are experiencing.

• Notice your calm breathing.... your relaxed muscles.... Enjoy the relaxation for a few moments....

• When you are ready to return to your usual level of alertness and awareness, slowly begin to re-awaken your body. Wiggle your toes and fingers. Swing your arms gently. Shrug your shoulders. Stretch if you like.

• You may now end this progressive muscle relaxation exercise feeling calm and refreshed.

# ASMR

ASMR stands for Autonomous Sensory Meridian Response, which is a relaxing and enjoyable tingling sensation that some people feel on their skin and scalp in response to certain stimuli. The formal recognition of it (along with the naming of it) came about on a message board in 2007, with a discussion on "head orgasms."

The associated research is brand new, but has already found ASMR to reduce heart rate and increase electrodermal response of the skin, which is the primary indicator of increased attention. It is thought to work on the same neural pathway that allows us to be soothed as babies and small children, using the light touch and gentle noises that help release endorphins, oxytocin, serotonin, and GABA.

Not everyone experiences it, probably only about 20% of us. (It may be a genetic mutation of sorts). If you experience ASMR you probably already know. If you aren't sure, look up a video and you'll be able to tell right away if it feels good or is just boring.

If ASMR relaxes you, you can add it to your self-soothing toolbox. A ton of people are out there making ASMR videos on youtube. If there is particular visual or aural content you are looking for, someone is creating that content. Or you can create the content yourself.

*Physical ASMR options you can try:* scalp tingler, hair brushing, massage,

*Audio ASMR options you can try:* tapping, wind blowing, paper crinkling, the sound of rain, a cat purring, a white noise machine

| Situation | SUDs before | ASMR technique | SUDs after |
| --- | --- | --- | --- |
| | | | |

# UNDERSTANDING YOUR MIND-BODY CONNECTION

Our bodies and brains really are not separate things, even though they are typically treated thusly. We tend to think of the body as the meat sack the brain is in charge of hauling around, when in fact they are as dynamic and interrelliant a duo as Grace and Frankie.

One of the major pathways of brain-body communication is the tenth cranial nerve, otherwise known as the vagus nerve, (historically referred to in Traditional Chinese Medicine as the du channel) which serves as the foundation of polyvagal theory. All methods of body-brain intercommunication appear to organize through this channel.

The vagus nerve is the part of us that most of the exercises in this book work on. It's the nerve that physically creates the mind-body connection, linking your brain and your gut and the rest of you. It's the body's communication system. It's how information, inflammation, and relaxation spread. And because our whole body is involved in our emotional health, understanding the vagus nerve helps us understand both our physical health and our emotions, and how they are connected. We're going to get into a ton of exercises that work to soothe and regulate the vagus nerve and gut, but first let's take a look at how we are feeling now.

# My Whole-Istic Personhood in the Here and Now

Let's start with getting a picture of how you feel right now. Figuring out how we actually feel—not just our emotions, but physically in our bodies, can be surprisingly difficult. But tuning into that is the first step to figuring out how to feel better.

First, we're going to think about various categories of our human experience, like sleep, nutrition, pain, and stress, and consider what 100% functionality would look like for us in each of these categories. Think big, but also keep in mind realistic constraints due to physical conditions, situational limitations, finances, etc. This is a pragmatic exercise, not a magic wand one. A 50 year old body won't be 20 years old again, an incurable medical condition can be managed but won't go away, and a two-month yoga retreat in Bali sounds amazing but probably isn't going to happen for most of us. But we can identify the best version of our physical and emotional selves within the laws of physics and the constraints of our pragmatic limitations.

We aren't looking at factors like weight loss, size loss, and appearance here, but functional outcomes like being able to enjoy playing kickball with your kids at the park, go on a hike with your friends, and waking up most mornings without feeling like an 18 wheeler broke into your house and drove over you while you were asleep.

Think about what is possible and probable and make that your 100%. Then fill in the thermometer on page 29 based on where you are right now, and keep filling it in as you work through the exercises in each area in the rest of this book.

## *REST AND DETOX (SLEEP)*

What does 100% look like for me?

What % am I at now?

What practical, manageable steps can I take to increase that?

## ENERGY AND HEALING SUPPORT (NUTRITION)

What does 100% look like for me?

What % am I at now?

What practical, manageable steps can I take to increase that?

## STRESS MANAGEMENT

What does 100% look like for me?

What % am I at now?

What practical, manageable steps can I take to increase that?

## PAIN MANAGEMENT

What does 100% look like for me?

What % am I at now?

What practical, manageable steps can I take to increase that?

## EMBODIED MOVEMENT

What does 100% look like for me?

What % am I at now?

What practical, manageable steps can I take to increase that?

## EMBODIED CENTERING (BREATHWORK/MINDFULNESS/MEDITATION)

What does 100% look like for me?

What % am I at now?

What practical, manageable steps can I take to increase that?

Is there any one area that needs the most attention, feels the most attainable, or that you generally want to tackle first? For what reasons does that one stand out?

100%

REST AND
DETOX (SLEEP)

0%

100%

ENERGY AND HEALING
SUPPORT (NUTRITION)

0%

100%

STRESS
MANAGEMENT

0%

100%

PAIN MANAGEMENT

0%

100%

EMBODIED MOVEMENT

0%

100%

EMBODIED CENTERING
(BREATHWORK/
MINDFULNESS/MEDITATION)

0%

# Symptoms Checklists

In *Unfuck Your Body*, I go into stress, trauma, inflammation, and toxicity as the four horsepeople of our bodily apocalypses. Holy shit, that's a terrible joke. But also mostly true, and either causes of or contributing factors to mood and anxiety disorders.

The exercises throughout this workbook should address each of these areas, including the specific chapters on trauma and stress. The vagus nerve exercises later on and the self-soothing and physical grounding things at the beginning of the book can be used to address the symptoms of all four.

These checklists of symptoms aren't meant to diagnose a disease, but if you have a big aha moment, please show your healthcare provider so they can look at further testing and diagnostic options.

## STRESS

### Physical Symptoms of Chronic Stress

○ Cardiovascular issues like abnormal heart rhythms, high blood pressure, heart disease, heart attacks, and strokes

○ Disordered eating patterns and and weird weight fluctuations due to jacked up hunger signals from cortisol

○ Menstrual problems

○ Loss of sexual desire, sexual dysfunction, impotence, and premature ejaculation

○ Problems with hair and skin (hair falling out, skin problems like rashes, eczema, acne, etc.)

○ Gut upset (IBS, gastritis, ulcers, nausea, GERD, etc.)

○ Low energy

○ Headaches, other aches and pains (chronic or acute), and tenseness throughout the body

○ Upset stomach, including diarrhea, constipation, and nausea

○ Racing heart and rapid breathing

○ Other nervous behaviors (fidgeting, picking at cuticles, etc)

- ○ Changes in sleep
- ○ Changes in appetite
- ○ Getting sick more easily than usual (colds, flus, infections)

## Emotional/Mental Stuff

- ○ Mental health problems, such as depression, anxiety, PTSD, and thought disorders
- ○ Feelings of agitation and frustration
- ○ Uncontrolled mood swings, racing thoughts
- ○ Thinking you are losing control, being out of control
- ○ Low level depression, hopelessness, helplessness, worthlessness
- ○ Unable to relax or enjoy things you usually enjoy
- ○ Avoiding people and situations you generally enjoyed in the past
- ○ Inability to focus, feeling disorganized and forgetful
- ○ Incessant worry
- ○ Making bad choices and judgements
- ○ Always framing things through a negative lens
- ○ Struggling to stay organized and/or focus your attention
- ○ Procrastinating and avoiding responsibilities
- ○ Increased use of substances to manage mood (drugs, alcohol, nicotine, caffeine)

## HPA-D Symptoms (Adrenal Fatigue)

- ○ Difficulty getting up in the morning
- ○ High levels of fatigue each day
- ○ Inability to handle stress (small things get really big, really fast)
- ○ Cravings for salty foods
- ○ Higher energy levels in the evenings (and not just because you are finally away from your stupid job or school day)
- ○ Overuse of stimulants like caffeine (I feel attacked)
- ○ A weak immune system (every bug that makes the rounds, you get)

## TOXIC OVERLOAD

Some physical signs that you might be dealing with a greater toxic load than your body can handle include:

- ○ Fatigue
- ○ Concentration difficulties
- ○ Muscle aches
- ○ Headaches
- ○ Joint pain
- ○ Sinus problems (congestion and/or postnasal drip)
- ○ Gas, bloating, water retention, constipation, diarrhea, or extra stinky poops[1]
- ○ Heartburn
- ○ Sleep problems
- ○ Food cravings (quick carbs usually because blood sugar is wonky)
- ○ Trouble losing weight, toning up, or increasing energy (you're doing the right things but your body isn't feeling any better)
- ○ Skin problems (rashes, eczema, psoriasis, acne, canker sores)
- ○ Halitosis
- ○ Puffy, dark circles under the eyes
- ○ Premenstrual syndrome or other menstrual disorders

## CHRONIC INFLAMMATION

Acute inflammation is pretty obvious, right? Pain, swelling, redness, heat, and complete loss of function. Chronic inflammation is more subtle.

**Stuff you might notice**

- ○ Fatigue
- ○ Sore joints
- ○ Chest pain
- ○ Lower back pain

---

1 I mean, all poop stinks. It's poop. But that chronic "something crawled up my ass and died" smell may mean toxins your body is working to dispel.

- Mouth sores
- Rashes (Livedo Reticularis, a purple marble-y rash is especially common)
- Insulin resistance (which you will notice either through checking your blood sugar or recognizing it in your body when it's unstable)
- Muscle weakness (myositis)
- Bowel inflammation (abdominal pain, diarrhea, cramping, constipation)
- Dry eye
- Mental fog
- Memory issues

**Stuff your doctor might notice**
- Hardening of the arteries (arteriosclerosis)
- Excessive blood clotting (hypercoagulation)
- Insulin resistance noted in bloodwork (high fasting glucose, high fasting triglycerides, high A1Cs (amount of red blood cells that have sugar coated hemoglobin)
- Increase in erythrocyte sedimentation rate (ESR), C-reactive protein (CRP) and plasma viscosity (PV) in your blood work (they demonstrate elevated protein, which is related to higher levels of inflammation)

## *TRAUMA*

I realize it's pretty weird of me to talk about the "bigness" of trauma responses and how diverse they are and how unique they are to our own circumstances. At the same time, many of these responses fall into certain categories. And manymanyMANY people are unaware that what they are doing is trauma response related. Meaning it's a safety adaptation that their brains came up with in light of everything they've been through. So as general and incomplete as it may be, it's still a really important starting point

**Reliving the Trauma Symptoms**
- Feeling like you are reliving the trauma even though it's behind you and you are physically safe. Not just thinking about it, but your body is reacting as if it is happening in the present.
- Dreaming that you are back in the traumatic event (or maybe a similar event).

○ Having a huge emotional response when something or someone reminds you about the trauma. Like freaking the fuck out, even though you are currently safe and/or having lots of physical symptoms (sweating, heart racing, fainting, breathing problems, headaches, etc.)

## Avoiding the Memories of the Trauma Symptoms

○ Doing things to distract from thoughts or feelings about the trauma, and/or avoiding talking about it when it comes up.

○ Avoiding things associated with the trauma, like people, places, and activities. And a lot of times these areas of avoidance get bigger and bigger. Like avoiding a certain street that an accident happened on. Then the whole neighborhood, then driving in a car at all.

○ Needing to feel in control in all circumstances, like sitting in places that feel safest in public places, not having close physical proximity with other people, avoiding crowds.

○ Having a hard time remembering important aspects of the trauma (blocking shit out).

○ Feeling totally numbed out or detached from everything or just about everything.

○ Not being interested in regular activities and fun stuff. Not being able to enjoy shit, even if it should be enjoyable shit.

○ Not being connected to your feelings and moods in general. Feeling just . . . blank.

○ Not seeing a future for yourself, like just more of the same versus things getting better.

## Other Medical or Emotional Symptoms

○ Stomach upset, trouble eating, only craving foods that are sugary (therefore more comforting to a stressed out body)

○ Continuously stressed out, and unregulated and out of your zone of tolerance for most of the time or all of the time.

○ Trouble falling asleep or staying asleep. Or sleeping a lot but for shit. Either way, feeling fucking exhausted all the time. Having intrusive traumatic dreams even in your sleep.

- Not having enough fucks in your pocket to take care of yourself in important ways (exercising, eating healthy foods, getting regular health care, safer sex with chosen partners).

- Soothing symptoms away with substances (e.g., drugs, alcohol, nicotine use, food) or behaviors (e.g., gambling, shopping, or dumb endorphin-producing shit like playing chicken with trains).

- Getting sick more frequently, or noticing that chronic physical health issues are getting worse.

- Anxiety, depression, guilt, edginess, irritability, and/or anger. (A *huge* number of mental health diagnoses are really just a trauma response that is not being properly treated, sadly.)

## PTSD SYMPTOMS

If you don't get a chance to process your trauma, it can turn into Post-Traumatic Stress Disorder in the long term (especially if you have a history of fucked up things happening in your life). There is a ton of research that shows that people who have been through something awful may not have PTSD in the ensuing months, but do quality for that diagnosis a year or so down the road.

- **Arousal** – The amygdala is always wearing its crazy pants and you find yourself freaked out when you shouldn't be or don't want to be. You may or may not know why. Your heart is racing, your breathing gets weird, your muscles get tense—you are shifting out of your zone of tolerance.

- **Avoidance** – You find yourself avoiding things that trigger arousal. Grocery store was bad? I can order my groceries online. Really don't need to leave the house for groceries, right?

- **Intrusion** – Thoughts, images, and memories related to the trauma experience start shoving their way up. The things that your brain was protecting you from don't actually go away. And they start bubbling to the surface without your consent or willingness. This isn't the same as rumination, where you worry over a bad memory intentionally; instead, stuff shows up when least expected. And you can't manage everything that is bubbling up.

- **Negative Thoughts and Feelings** – With all this other stuff going on is it any wonder that you never feel good? Or even just okay?

## SYMPTOMS OF ANXIETY

Anxiety is an emotional response that shows itself in mental and very physical ways. Here are some of the things that might look like. Some people might have all these experiences, other people might have a few, or different ones at different times.

You are probably reading the physical body checklist and thinking . . . this is the same list for everything from anxiety to Ebola. Which is why so many people end up in emergency rooms thinking they are having a heart attack when they are having an anxiety attack. It's *also* the same reason many people have missed the fact that they were having a heart attack because they were also having an anxiety attack. It's important to have any possible medical conditions ruled out because so many physical health issues can look like mental health issues.

**Thoughts and Feelings Symptoms**

- Excessive worry
- Rumination (hamster wheel thinking patterns)
- Irritability/anger (Weird, right? Anger is the culturally allowed emotion so we substitute that one a lot for what we are really feeling)
- Irrational fears/specific phobias
- Stage fright/social phobias
- Hyper self-awareness/self-consciousness
- Feelings of fear
- A sense of helplessness
- Flashbacks
- Obsessive behaviors, pickiness
- Compulsive behaviors
- Self doubt
- A sense that you are "losing it" or "going crazy"

**Physical Body Symptoms**

- Trouble falling asleep or staying asleep
- Inability to rest

- ○ Muscle tension
- ○ Neck tension
- ○ Chronic indigestion
- ○ Stomach pain and/or nausea
- ○ Racing heart
- ○ Pulsing in the ear (feeling your heartbeat)
- ○ Coldness, numbness or tingling in toes, feet, hands, or fingers
- ○ Sweating
- ○ Weakness
- ○ Shortness of breath
- ○ Dizziness
- ○ Lightheadedness
- ○ Chest pain
- ○ Feeling hot and cold (feeling like having chills and fever without running a temperature)
- ○ Shooting pains/feeling like you have had an electric shock

**Other symptoms**

- ○ Perfectionism
- ○ Indecisiveness
- ○ Brain fog
- ○ Depersonalization
- ○ Avoidance
- ○ Fatigue
- ○ Low tolerance

## SYMPTOMS OF DEPRESSION

Depression is a physical illness. Everything that we discuss as "mental illness" just means brain-based physical illness. And depression isn't even fully brain based. It's especially interrelated with both trauma and inflammation, so it fully makes sense to discuss depression symptomology in the context of this workbook.

### Dysthymia (Persistent Depressive Disorder)

Dysthymia is like perpetually wearing gloom-covered glasses. People with dysthymia are more likely to function better in daily life and seem more okay to outside observers than people with Major Depressive Disorder. But they aren't really human-ing at a fundamental level. If you have dysthymia, you may have periods of OK-ness, but those periods generally don't last for more than a month or two before the motherfucker is back on your couch, eating all your chips again.

Symptoms of dysthymia can include:

- Less interest, or no interest, in daily activities
- Feeling sad, or down, or just kind of empty
- Feeling pretty hopeless about life
- Low energy, feeling low-level tired all the time (whether getting sleep or not)
- Feeling like you can't do shit right, having lots of negative self-talk or low self-esteem that isn't really related to reality (because while saying you are bad at dunking when you're 4'11" is likely legit, saying you are fundamentally broken, shitty, and unlovable isn't)
- Trouble paying attention, concentrating, or making decisions
- Anger or irritability
- Serious decrease in productivity of effective task completion
- Avoiding social situations and activities (the ones you would actually like to do in theory, or used to like to do)
- Worry, guilt, or shame
- Changes in eating (either overeating or not wanting to eat at all)
- Changes in sleep patterns (sleeping too much, not sleeping enough, sleeping badly)
- Stuck in the past and negative experiences that happened

## Major Depressive Disorder (MDD)

An actual diagnosis of major depressive disorder requires that anhedonia (which is that lack of connection and enjoyment in life) be present every day for at least two weeks. Other symptoms that are also really, really common are:

- Loss of interest in all the things fun, excellent, and the point of being human (anhedonia, like I mentioned above)
- Low energy/fatigue
- Low-level chronic pain
- Headaches, stomach pain, or chest pain
- Jacked up concentration, difficulty making decisions
- Feeling guilty and/or worthless
- Sleeping a ton or sleeping for shit (not sleeping at all, or sleeping badly)
- Feeling either super restless or really slowed down (like moving underwater or brain wrapped in cotton)
- Intrusive thoughts of death (morbid ideation) or suicide (suicidal ideation)
- Change in eating habits (and 5% or more change in weight, either up or down, because of it)
- Irritability, anger, low distress tolerance

## Bipolar Disorder

Then there is bipolar disorder (which used to be called manic-depression).

People who have bipolar disorder cycle through highs and lows. It's not depression and non-depression, but depression and mania, an intensely elevated mood. It's not necessarily fun and happy—it can also be high agitation, irritability, and anger. Unlike normal levels of elevated emotions, mania takes us over completely. Someone in a manic state really struggles to control their actions because their brains are in over-fire—no passing go, no collecting two hundred dollars.

Mania can cause other symptoms as well, but some of the key signs of this phase of bipolar disorder are:

- Racing thoughts

- ○ Talking really fast
- ○ Not needing much sleep to function
- ○ Being easily distracted
- ○ Feeling really restless
- ○ Acting impulsively
- ○ Being confident in your abilities far beyond your actual skills
- ○ Elevated mood (either super high and happy or super angry and irritable)
- ○ Making poor decisions/choices, engaging in risky behaviors (like with sex or money)
- ○ Break from reality (psychosis)

## Personal Symptom Record

Anxiety, depression, and trauma don't show up on lab tests. Toxicity, inflammation, and stress might, but only if we're testing for those issues. To get help for them, you'll usually need to get your own damn self into a clinic or doctor's office saying "shit is fucked and I really really need to figure this out and get help" so that someone can help you sort through the shit and figure out what's wrong. And that's what this worksheet is for. Not for you to self-diagnose and then demand Xanax from your doc, but for you to take time to create a good record of what's been going on so you can connect with a clinician who can ask good questions, clarify information, and help you figure out what treatment and support you need… and hopefully in far less than ten fucking years. So consider using this and bringing it in to your appointment and requesting to go through it with your treatment provider.

What *does* "symptom" mean? Anything that you are thinking, feeling, or doing that is reinforcing problems or stuckness in your life instead of growth and healing.

| Symptom | Intensity (1-10) | How long does it last? | How many times per week? | For how many months/years? |
|---------|------------------|------------------------|--------------------------|----------------------------|
|         |                  |                        |                          |                            |
|         |                  |                        |                          |                            |
|         |                  |                        |                          |                            |
|         |                  |                        |                          |                            |

# UNDERSTAND YOUR TRAUMA

**S**hort answer: It's trauma. It's always the fucking trauma. Trauma is something I write about a lot—it's the whole point of these books.

When we talk about our five senses, we talk about how we use them to organize information from the outside world, but rarely do we use them to register what is going on inside of us. In reality, we are receiving internal sensory information on a constant basis but are rarely connected to that experience simply because that's how bodies are supposed to act. *All of it.* Walking, talking, breathing, avoiding a crack in the concrete that we could trip over, recognizing that the milk is spoiled as soon as we open the container and not drinking it. It would take too much of our physical and mental effort to do all of these things consciously and continuously. These behaviors have to be automatic for our survival.

But what if the correction process has become trauma informed?

Sometimes the wiring goes wonky. You know. Our body and mind are over-eager and over-protective and start sending haywire messages that are overanalyzing current experiences and anticipating dangerous and damaging future experiences based on our past experiences.

That's the very definition of a trauma response.

Any living animal will respond to changes in light and shadow. From amoebas to Homo sapiens, we perceive threat and duck. The difference between us and amoebas is that we can (at least on a good day), become aware of our instincts and challenge the efficacy of our ducking patterns. This means being more aware of the interplay between our external and internal sense messages. And learning to tolerate our duck response without needing to always duck.

We need this duck response to survive. But sometimes it gets stuck on.

And when it sticks around for the long term, we call it PTSD, which is a fear response that gets switched on but never gets switched off.

PTSD can come from one specific terrible event, which is what the psychological establishment defines it as, but it also can come from a ton of bad things adding up.

Trauma and PTSD are widely recognized as a major factor in our mental health. But they are very much bodily reactions, which is why this book exists.

## Unpacking Our Trauma with ACEs

Of course, trauma affects our health at all stages of life, but childhood trauma is more likely to change our epigenetic structure, according to a 2014 Yale University study. The world is unsafe from the get-go, and when things happen to us as kids—either one big event or a lot of bad things—our stress response gets set to high alert, which can persist through our adult life if left untreated.

One term being thrown around on the regular now to account for the impact of childhood trauma on our bodies is "ACEs." An ACE is an "adverse childhood event" which is a fancy way of saying childhood trauma. The Center for Disease Control and Kaiser Permanente conducted one of the largest research studies on the impact of ACEs on health and well-being over the lifespan, and developed a questionnaire which is widely used for determining how much childhood trauma might be a part of your life now.

The ACE questions are looking for information about your life prior to your 18th birthday, specifically regarding, abuse, neglect, and what are termed *household challenges*. Abuse questions ask about physical, emotional, and sexual abuse. Neglect questions focus on physical and emotional neglect. And the household challenges include having family members with a mental illness and/or substance dependence, having family members incarcerated, witnessing interpersonal violence, or witnessing separation and/or divorce.

If you want, stop right here, do an internet search for "ACEs questionnaire" and see what your score is. My personal favorite is the California ACEs Aware version (it's the one that I have my interns train in using). It's owned by the people who paid for its development, so we can't reprint it here (I mean, fair), but it's widely available for individuals to assess themselves.

**Your ACEs score:**
Were there any surprises on that questionnaire? Anything you want to unpack more?

# Unpacking Our Bigger Picture Traumas

While ACEs has the most data behind it, and it is true that the earlier traumas we experience have the most lasting effects on our adult lives, the impact of traumatic events is bigger than the ACEs and bigger than the diagnostic and statistical manual we use to diagnose PTSD (DSM-5).These are just some of the things that can be a trauma. In the end, we all experience trauma differently, and are impacted by too many things to list. Creating a list that touches only on the big "diagnosable" categories dismisses other experiences that shouldn't be dismissed.

So the list below is intended to start conversations, and maybe help you realize the legitimacy of some life experiences as being traumatic. And while my list is more inclusive than one you will read in the DSM, it's still a general one. Your experiences may cross several categories even if it is a singular event, which is important to note as well. The list may not fit at all. Trauma doesn't operate by checking the right box in the right category. So I hope that you will believe me when I say *your experiences and reactions are valid and real and you are worthy of care and the opportunity to heal.*

Check the box next to any that you've experienced, and write a couple words to classify the event(s)

about any of these that you have experienced, like "the divorce" or "the accident." That's more than enough info because this is about recognizing the complexity of trauma in our lives, not writing out hugely detailed trauma narratives.

## CHILD ABUSE (PHYSICAL, SEXUAL, EMOTIONAL, NEGLECT)

Child abuse is a huge category, and even the federal government has struggled to define it well. But essentially, any act (or failure to act/intervene) that harms a child or puts a child at imminent risk of harm is abuse. The younger the child, the more powerless and fragile they are, the more limitations there are to them being able to defend themselves or outcry, the more risk there is for serious, ongoing abuse.

## DOMESTIC/INTIMATE PARTNER VIOLENCE (PHYSICAL, SEXUAL, EMOTIONAL, ECONOMIC, PSYCHOLOGICAL)

Domestic violence is the adult version of child abuse, for lack of a better comparison. It occurs in intimate partner/romantic relationships among both youth and adults. You do not have to be sharing a living space with your romantic partner for it to be considered domestic violence.

The US Department of Justice notes a few differences in the types of violence that can occur in intimate partner relationships, as opposed to child abuse. Emotional abuse includes attacks on the partner's self-worth (criticism, name-calling) while psychological abuse is more action-oriented, and can consist of isolating their partner, threatening harm to them or others that they care about, or destroying items that have meaning to them (without physically abusing them or other people). Economic abuse focuses on the way a partner creates a situation wherein they have all economic control in the relationship, forcing the abused partner to remain with them (controlling all money, or not letting them have a job or get job training, for example).

## ELDERLY/DISABLED ADULT ABUSE (PHYSICAL, SEXUAL, EMOTIONAL, NEGLECT, EXPLOITATION)

Adult individuals who are dependent to a certain extent on the care of others, or are otherwise considered at risk for abuse or neglect fall under this category. Unlike the above category, where the relationship is considered an equal one (until manipulated to be otherwise), some adults are considered by law to be powerless and fragile, and therefore have the same protections under the law that children are due. These individuals include older adults and individuals with physical or mental health impairments. The one main difference between child abuse and elderly/disabled abuse is the concept of exploitation. An adult with income (for example, social security or retirement income) may have the use of that income exploited by another individual. While many adults have individuals who help them manage their money effectively, making sure their needs are met, there are many other adults who go without basics because that money is being mismanaged by their "caretaker."

### ◌ IMPAIRED CAREGIVER

Unlike in the above cases, many individuals have caregivers who are not causing intentional harm or neglectful practices, but have their own impairments that make it difficult to render care, which can have a negative impact on the individuals they care for. For example, a child with a parent being treated for cancer may struggle with not having all their needs met due to the illness of the caretaker. This is coupled with the anxiety of seeing the illness and decline of the person who is their primary means of support and one of the people they love most in the world. Generally speaking, we are thinking of children when we are thinking of someone who may have an impaired caregiver, but an adult who has a disability that renders them reliant on the care of another could also be affected.

### ◌ SCHOOL VIOLENCE

School violence can consist of one-time, sentinel events (like a school shooting), or be the product of chronically dangerous school conditions (gang warfare, drug use, drug sales, fighting, etc.). If an individual is engaged in a school environment, and witnesses, partakes in, or is a victim of violence within it, that can be considered a traumatic event.

### ◌ COMMUNITY VIOLENCE

As with school violence, living or working in certain communities can also pose a risk for trauma exposure. We can experience one-time, sentinel events (again, such as a shooting), or be exposed to violence on a regular basis by the nature of the common experiences found in the community to which we are exposed (drug use, fighting, etc.). Most community violence can be tied to neighborhoods that have been left impoverished of hope, opportunity, and money. Many of the other categories could also fall under the broad category of "community violence," but are widespread enough to merit their own section.

## ⟡ BULLYING/CYBERBULLYING

Bullying, defined, is the use of one's strength or influence to control the actions of another. It can include real violence, the threat of violence, or intimidation to wield power over another. The traditional form of bullying is the older kid taking the lunch money of the younger one. But in the digital age bullying can take many different forms. Electronic communication allows new ways of bullying to take place—from a distance and with anonymity in an increasing number of cases. This has allowed individuals who wouldn't normally have power over our lives to wreak serious havoc.

The term "bullied" is often misused, to the point of being so commonplace that it is often dismissed. Someone expressing disagreement is not a form of bullying. Even if they are doing so loudly and annoyingly. Even if they are a total asshole about it. Being irritated by someone else's douchebaggery is not the same as being bullied.

Serious bullying experiences are often tied to a trauma response. Research I had done in my local community mental health agency demonstrated that an enormous portion of the children and youth that were brought to the mental health crisis center identified being bullied as the reason for their mental health crisis (often expressed in the form of suicidal or homicidal ideation). This reminded me at the time how incredibly important it is that we recognize the impact bullying can have on our emotional health and wellbeing.

## ⟡ SEXUAL VIOLENCE

Sexual violence often falls under the domain of child abuse or domestic partner violence. Other forms of sexual violence very well could fall under the heading of community violence.

Sexual violence crosses all cultural and economic barriers. Individuals are raped by known offenders 80% of the time, though many of these offenders are acquaintances, not intimate partners. And another 20% are complete strangers. (RAINN, 2015).

And according to Equality Now (2015), trafficking women and children for sexual exploitation is the fastest growing criminal enterprise in the world. At least 20.9 million adults and children (98% of which are women and girls) are bought and sold worldwide into commercial sexual servitude, forced labor and bonded labor. Approximately 10% are children, and the majority overall were trafficked for the sole intent of sexual exploitation.

## MEDICAL (ILLNESS OR ACCIDENT)

Whether a significant but short-term illness or a chronic condition, dealing with the negative impact of a health crisis can be intensely traumatic. There's the loss of function and freedom from the health problem itself, and then there's the stress of accessing needed care and struggling to pay for it. Individuals with chronic, debilitating diseases which can be treated but not cured have to struggle with coming to terms with a "new normal," and many know that this disease will eventually no longer be treatable—and the decline accompanying that experience is terrifying.

## NATURAL OR HUMAN-MADE DISASTERS

Natural disasters are events such as tornados, earthquakes, and floods that wreak havoc on our communities. Man-made disasters have a similar impact, but are the result of human action or inaction (such as industrial accidents like Chernobyl or the Exxon Valdez spill). There can be significant overlap between the two, as failure in planning for or engaging in appropriate action during or after a natural disaster worsens the consequences, leaking into being a man-made disaster (i.e., studies of the Hurricane Katrina floods demonstrate that the majority of the flooding was due to faulty levees installed by the US Army Corps of Engineers, not the hurricane itself).

## WAR/TERRORISM

The standard definitions of these terms assume that war is engaged in between willing participants with agreed-upon terms, while terrorism is conducted by renegades and targets innocent bystanders. Clearly, this isn't an accurate definition . . . however, the perception of one form of violence being more acceptable than the other has often led to a lack of understanding about the trauma inherent in both.

While we expect and empathize with the suffering of the innocent bystander, the individuals who willingly serve as soldiers are also likely to struggle with PTSD or other trauma-related symptoms. According to the VA, 10-30% of US soldiers have suffered PTSD sometime during their return home after being in a conflict (the statistics vary based on the service era). The US Department of Veterans Affairs released a statistic in 2013, citing approximately 22 veteran suicides occurring per day. No matter our role in such situations, the impact can be devastating.

## FORCED DISPLACEMENT

We are sometimes forced to leave the only place we have known as home. Oftentimes these reasons are for our own safety, but it can still be traumatic. It is important to remember that whether you are leaving war-torn Syria as a refugee or being placed in a foster home due to a parent's inability to provide adequate care, leaving your home and community is a trauma in and of itself. No matter how dire the circumstances, being placed in new and unfamiliar surroundings and leaving the only home you have ever known requires a huge shift in thinking and behavior that is intensely difficult.

## TRAUMATIC GRIEF/BEREAVEMENT

While grief is a normal part of the human experience, some people struggle with intense loss in such a way that their response develops in line with that of other traumatic events, and they are unable to process the loss in a way that allows them to move forward.

## SYSTEMS TRAUMA

Individuals who are subject to the mechanizations of some sort of system are also at risk for a trauma response. For example, children in foster care or the juvenile justice system may struggle with the trauma associated with the events that resulted in their entering the system, the trauma of the displacement experience, and *then* the continued trauma of having very little power and control over their experience within the system. Not knowing what your future will look like, being unable to form support networks due to continued movement and staff turnover, and not being able to obtain accurate information about your situation are all common experiences. The health care system, the legal system, the immigration system, or any other giant system that has control over your life can result in trauma, and may have been reinforced and/or worsened by structural racism, ablism, sexism, monosexism, heterosexism, gender binarism, etc. A system itself often perpetuates its own, ongoing form of trauma that cannot be discounted when we look at the experiences that shape us.

## INTERGENERATIONAL TRAUMA

Historical oppression and its consequences are often transmitted down generations. This can happen through continued poverty and lack of opportunity in communities (such as Indian reservations), as well as within our literal genetic code. Trauma experienced by our parents and grandparents has the capacity to change our epigenetic structure (our gene expression) in utero, causing many individuals to be born with a hardwired trauma response. Ongoing structural trauma against groups of people doesn't generally operate as a "new" traumatic event, but a reinforcement/continuation of ancestral trauma.

Did any of the items you checked stand out for you as needing further exploration? Did any surprise you? Do certain events resound in more than one category?

# Trauma Safety Plan

Some traumatic events hit us in such a way that we don't recover with time. And our brains encode that experience as an ongoing experience, and then tries to protect us by holding onto every possible sign that something might hurt us in the way we've been hurt in the past. And it doesn't take much for the switch to get flipped... places, people, smells, tones of voice, or even our thoughts.

As you've maybe already experienced, the topics in this book have the ability to bring up a lot of pain and old traumas. Especially if the reasons we've been behaving out of line with our values are themselves based in trauma. So let's look at how traume reactivates so we can create better strategies for working through these events.

So what's the mechanism of activating that old trauma script? It's a trigger, just like smelling hot buttered popcorn is a trigger for your salivary glands. A trigger is something that facilitates reliving a traumatic event. A trigger is something in the present that activates our memories of a past trauma in such a way that we are reliving that past moment in our present experience.

For example, a car brake squealing can make the brain freak out and make you think that you are getting hit by a car again. Or someone wearing the same scent as an abusive authority figure in your childhood can make all those feelings of anger or helplessness come back. That is your brain warning you that you might be in danger. It doesn't make you crazy, it makes you a survivor.

But it also means you are no longer in the present moment, dealing with present stimuli. It means your brain is playing the tape of whatever terrible shit happened to you in the past as a mechanism of trying to protect you in the present. Your brain just doesn't understand that the present is probably not as scary or dangerous as the recording.

Sometimes we limit ourselves by avoiding all possible triggers, which makes protective sense, but then we never heal. . And it's a crappy way to live and you deserve better. Instead, let's work on figuring out what's going on and developing new ways of being so we can live the lives we want for ourselves.

Use the next three exercises to evaluate your triggers and figure out what sets them off and the most effective ways to manage them.

Once you start putting a formal plan into place to manage your triggers, you will notice some stuff works great, some stuff not at all, and new ideas may come up that you want to incorporate. You may also get feedback from the people you love and trust. Make any notes that you want to remember here, too.

**When you are feeling the most healthy, happy, joyful, and well what does life look like?** *How do you spend your days? How do you feel? How do you interact with others? What do you like to do?*

**What things have you noticed help you manage your triggers more effectively in a general sense?** *How much sleep do you need? How much exercise is beneficial? What should you be eating? Do you need to pray, meditate, or see certain people more/less often? What activities help?*

**What things from this list can you commit to doing regularly to help maintain equilibrium?** *List 1-5 things you aren't doing regularly right now that you know would really help.*

**What are some of the situations that you have come to realize are triggers for you?** *Rather than big, catastrophic things, think of things that happen on a more regular basis. E.g. "being in a crowded room" or "not doing well on a project," holidays or birthdays, smells, sounds, or voices. We don't know all of our triggers and may get triggered without any idea of what caused it but if you keep notes, you can often figure them out. Consider this list a work in progress.*

**What are your early warning signs that you may be getting triggered?** *What kinds of thoughts do you have? What emotions arise? What kind of behaviors do you engage in that you don't typically do?*

**If you are triggered, what are the things you can do for yourself to help you manage your response to these triggers?** *These are things you already do that become especially important in these situations but may also be coping skills or activities that you use when you are in especially tough situations. Faith wrote a whole book on the subject, Coping Skills.*

**What do you need from others in terms of support?** *You need help from others, especially if you are working on your intimate relationships. Who do you trust to provide that support? How will you ask them about it?*

**How will you know that you have been triggered past the point that you, and the individuals who traditionally support you, can handle?** *What will you notice in terms of your behaviors? Your feelings? Your thoughts? What should you and the people who support you watch out for?*

**If you are at a point at which you are not able to manage these triggers on your own, or with the assistance of the people who traditionally support you, what is the next step for you?** *Do you have treatment professionals that should be contacted? Crisis lines you prefer? A hospital you prefer, if needed? What resources are available to provide additional support?*

**Once your crisis has been managed, how will you know when you are feeling safe and secure again?** *What does restabilization look like for you? How can you communicate that to the people who may be worried about you?*

## Types of Triggers

Now that we have a plan for how to manage being triggered, it can be helpful to go a bit deeper and figure out what our different types of triggers are.

**True Triggers:** That pre-thought wordless terror. It's a body based, felt-sense reaction that we often don't even recognize until after the fact. The best way to handle a true trigger is to simply notice its existence and use skills to ground ourselves and bring our bodies back to safety.

**Distressing Reminders:** These are things that call up memories of the trauma and cause awful feelings but through which we can still think and function. A lot of times we can describe what we are feeling even if we can't explain it. The best way to handle a distressing reminder is to soothe yourself when you are experiencing it.

**Uncomfortable Associations:** These occur when something that would otherwise be pleasant or at least neutral has an association to our trauma. We are able to manage these associations by consciously reframing them.

# Trigger Response Plan

Now that you have an idea about the different types of triggers you are experiencing, you can create a plan to manage them. Practicing coping while you are not being triggered will help you remember what works when you need to. Try using coping and grounding skills from the introduction exercises that are specific to your types of triggers and rate how they worked so you can start to develop a more specific plan of attack for dealing with them.

## True Triggers

| Trigger | Coping Skill | Effectiveness |
| --- | --- | --- |
| | | |

## Distressing Reminders

| Trigger | Coping Skill | Effectiveness |
| --- | --- | --- |
| | | |

## Uncomfortable Associations

| Trigger | Coping Skill | Effectiveness |
| --- | --- | --- |
| | | |

# UNFUCK YOUR MIND-BODY CONNECTION

O ur bodies and brains really are not separate things, even though they are typically treated thusly. We tend to think of the body as the meat sack the brain is in charge of hauling around, when in fact they are as dynamic and interrelliant a duo as Grace and Frankie.

One of the major pathways of brain-body communication is the tenth cranial nerve, otherwise known as the vagus nerve, (historically referred to in Traditional Chinese Medicine as the du channel) which serves as the foundation of polyvagal theory. All methods of body-brain intercommunication appear to organize through this channel.

The vagus nerve is the part of us that most of this book rests on. It's the nerve that physically creates the mind-body connection, linking your brain and your gut and the rest of you. It's the body's communication system. It's how information, inflammation, and relaxation spread. And because our whole body is involved in our emotional health, understanding the vagus nerve helps us understand both our physical health and our emotions, and how they are connected. In the next part of the book, we'll look at trauma, inflammation, stress, and toxicity and how the vagus nerve mediates them all.

The vagus nerve's information flow is designed to help us stay alive and stay safe. But like every other safety process, it is designed to err on the side of caution by embedding memories of past threats and overcorrecting *juuuuuuust* in case something might be dangerous. Hence, the prevalence of trauma-informed responses and fuckery galore.

So back in the intro I promised that if you haven't read the book, I would make sure you got all the info you need to do the exercises? That's what this info is here. The deep dive into not only how it works but how it interacts with toxicity, inflammation, and stress is in *Unfuck Your Body*, if you're a science nerd like that. But for now, the key thing you need to know is about our fight-flight-freeze response, which is in many ways regulated by our vagus nerve.

The sympathetic nervous system governs our fight-flight-freeze instinct, which is critical to our survival. It is activated in the face of a threat or perceived threat, whether it be to our actual, physical safety, the individuals we love and care for, our possessions, or our needs, wants, desires, well-being, and belief systems. Essentially, anything that challenges the core of who and what we are and who or what belongs to us invokes a protective response. It has nothing to do with how mentally or physically strong we are or how much we love the person or people that we are with. That ability to be engaged and connected goes offline. If we perceive aggression as a means of escape, we will fight. If our instincts tell us we can't fight effectively but we can escape, we will flee. If neither of these responses are likely going to be effective, we will freeze.

Flight, fight, and freeze reactions are essential to our survival. But these are the threat reactions that get stuck in the "on" position when we are traumatized, like we talked about in the last chapter. Learning what it feels like when we are experiencing these reactions, and learning to move back out of them easily is half the battle.

## Recognizing Your Personal Vagal Responses

Our body's vagal response has an array of "options." Visualize a series of light switches, with "safe" in the middle and "too low" on one end and "too high" on the other, and a couple of switches in between for when you're moving down or up.

Stephen Porges, who brought vagal theory into mainstream psychology, visualizes the response options as existing on a ladder, which presumes that we enter and exit certain states in a certain order. I've found this personally confusing and prefer to visualize a series of flip-switch options rather than a spectrum.

Depending on the level of threat detected and previous experiences, the body

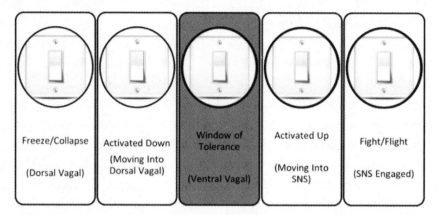

| Freeze/Collapse | Activated Down | Window of Tolerance | Activated Up | Fight/Flight |
|---|---|---|---|---|
| (Dorsal Vagal) | (Moving Into Dorsal Vagal) | (Ventral Vagal) | (Moving Into SNS) | (SNS Engaged) |

will flip one switch rather than another which is why you can go from fight/flight to complete collapse so quickly. The body has to make snap decisions. I have worked with people who only freeze up, others who only fight, and people who run the gamut. Remember how I mentioned earlier it's about what the body recognizes is its best bet for survival or pain management?

On the "too low" end of the spectrum, you have the freeze/collapse response switch, scientifically known as the Dorsal Vagal response. On either end is the sympathetic nervous system switch. On the "too high" end, you've got your fight and flight responses, or as we call it "SNS-engaged." In the safe center, you have your window of tolerance switch, where your vagus nerve sees no threat and your parasympathetic nervous system is engaged. That's your baby bear just right switch. Like any spectrum, there are shades in between—you can be activated down into dorsal vagal or moving up into SNS and notice that and bring yourself back into your window of tolerance if you need to. That's what we'll be working on here.

Our goal is to stay within our window of tolerance, and learn to expand our window of tolerance as much as possible. In a perfect world, we would become activated enough to deal with potentially threatening situations, but we wouldn't become SNS-engaged or dorsal vagal unless we were under a real attack, right? But a trauma response trains our bodies to presume attack based on the traumas we experienced. So it may not be real in an external world sense, but is very real to our internal world.

## WINDOW OF TOLERANCE

In our our window of tolerance state (ventral vagal), our muscles are relaxed, our breathing is easy, our heart rate is resting, our blood pressure is normal, our skin is our "normal" rosy hue (which is obvs different for everyone, but there is blood flow to the skin enough to give us some color), our pupils are normal sized, our eyelids are relaxed, and our digestion is functioning. Our eyes and mouth are moist and our skin is dry. We can differentiate individual sounds from background noise (the muscles of our middle ear have tone). Emotionally we are calm. We can feel love and pleasure. More complex emotions are bearable (e.g, we can be sad or frustrated but process through the experience with a sense of it being manageable). Our prefrontal cortex (thinking brain) is engaged. We are able to connect with self and others, and feel integrated within our own bodies. Our parasympathetic nervous system is in charge and it's doing a great job.

What signs tell you that you are in your window of tolerance?

What activities, coping skills, and behaviors help you remain in your window of tolerance? Which can you do for yourself? Which do you need support from others to do? Who are your go-to support people?

## FIGHT / FLIGHT

As we start getting into the the danger zone heading toward fight or flight (with our sympathetic nervous system activated), our muscles become more tense, our breathing gets faster and comes more from our upper chest (hyperventilation), our heart rate and blood pressure go up, our skin gets paler (under whatever level of melanation we have) because blood is rushing to our muscles away from the skin, our pupils become dilated, our eyelids get tense, and our digestion halts (this is why the dorsal vagal is called fight/flight and ventral vagal is referred to as rest/digest). Our eyes and mouth start to become dry while our skin starts to get sweaty (though it may be a cold sweat). Sounds become overwhelming, and it becomes harder to pick out individual voices (we lose tone in the muscles in our middle ear to make it easier to pick out low frequency predator sounds). Emotionally, we start to feel angry or fearful and our ability to connect with others becomes increasingly limited and eventually not likely. Concomitantly, our thinking brain goes increasingly offline and we find it more and more difficult to connect to our own bodies.

What signs tell you that you are in fight or flight mode?

What helps you move out of this response and back into your window of tolerance? Which can you do for yourself? Which do you need support from others to do? Who are your go-to support people?

## FREEZE / COLLAPSE

As we move into the shutdown state of freeze mode (dorsal vagal activated), our muscles become rigid instead of tense, and we will move from hyperventilation (getting too much oxygen) into hypoventilation. Our breathing and heart rate can bottom out to very slow (bradycardiac). Our blood pressure will also get very high and then bottom out. Our skin will often become even paler, our pupils get very small, our eyelids will start to move from very tense to either completely closed or stuck open. Our eyes and mouth will get very dry and our skin may go from extremes of hot to cold, though will eventually become very cold if we continue in this state. All auditory stimuli can become loud and overwhelming and you may shut all sound out completely because of it. Emotionally, we may feel terror or complete dissociation. Our thinking brain moves into being inaccessible, and connection with others and our own bodies moves to being impossible.

> NOTE: Once you are in hypofreeze (bradycardia) this is now a medical emergency, and emergency medical care is required. You've probably heard about seeking medical attention if someone is "in shock" and that's exactly what's going on here.

What signs tell you that you are in freeze mode?

What helps you move out of this response and back into your window of tolerance? Which can you do for yourself? Which do you need support from others to do? Who are your go-to support people?

## VAGAL RESPONSE LOG

The exercises in the rest of the book are pretty much all about training your brain to recognize when something isn't a true emergency, expanding your window of tolerance, and shortening the amount of time you spend out of it. Even just being aware of your vagal responses can help you manage them better. So let's keep track of how often a vagal response gets triggered, and how long it lasts before you return to your window of tolerance.

| Date | Triggering Event | Vagal Response | Time Activated | Techniques Tried |
|------|------------------|----------------|----------------|------------------|
|      |                  |                |                |                  |

## CHART YOUR VAGAL RESPONSE

As you do this work, you'll spend less and less time outside your window of tolerance. Sometimes it's hard to see this happening, even when you're only getting annoyed by something that you would have reduced you to a puddle a year ago. Here's a place to keep track of your progress over a longer period of time so you can see growth.

Each week, keep track of the number of times you leave your window of tolerance and write that number below. After three months, see what's changed.

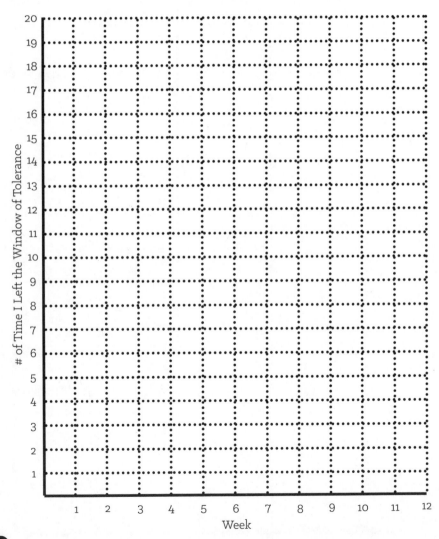

# Ear Stuff

The most direct way to improve your vagal tone is through stimulating the auricular branch of the vagus nerve (ABVN) which runs through the skin of the outer ear canal and parts of the ear. I know this seems like a weird place to be able to access the vagus nerve directly through the body, but that's because it's actually a remnant of our embryonic nerve, which supplied the first branchial arch.

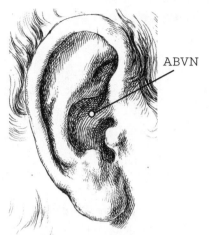

ABVN

It is also known as Alderman's nerve, a century's old historic reference to London politicians who would activate the ABVN with rosewater to encourage digestion. Besides helping with indigestion, stimulating the ABVN has shown to help with migraines, panic attacks, and our stress response. Stimulating the ABVN is being investigated as a medical intervention for chronic heart failure, so it's the real deal. This impacts the vagus nerve directly, telling the body to activate the parasympathetic response system again, which puts us back in our window of tolerance.

If you are looking at an ear, and consider the ear canal 12 o'clock, the ABVN runs 1 to 3 o'clock from it. You can feel the cartilage from the ABVN which leads down to the ear canal if you are poking your finger around in there, looking like a weirdo in the middle of the grocery store.

Pressing on that area or wearing an ear seed (an acupressure ball that you stick onto your skin) are both ways of stimulating the ABVN. I also know several people who have had that area pierced and found it hugely beneficial for their anxiety and migraine headaches. I'm not recommending ABVN piercing necessarily (an ear seed is way less invasive), but if you were kind of wanting to get one anyway it may have benefits beyond the aesthetic.

# Tongue Stuff

The tongue is so weird, y'all. The deeper we get into this, the weirder the body seems to be. The tongue is part of the autonomic nervous system *and* part of what is called the somatic nervous system, which is a whole entire nervous system devoted to the parts of our body that are under conscious control. So the tongue is activated both consciously and unconsciously. And it is thought to be part of all three components of the autonomic nervous system. Not just the sympathetic and parasympathetic, but also the enteric—which makes sense, because our tongues are an essential part of our eating and digestive process. The tongue represents the gateway to the enteric system, due to the presence of specialized ganglia on the anterior and posterior area of the tongue; it would act as a chemical "spy," letting the stomach know what fuckery we have put in our mouths.

And remember when I talked about the difference between afferent and efferent information?

Meaning brain-to-body and body-to-brain communication? The tongue becomes a crossroads of efferent *and* afferent information.

Because the tongue operates involuntarily and voluntarily, this is another place we can activate vagal tone. One of the simplest ways is tongue positioning. When we push our tongue up against the roof of our mouth (even if we do it subconsciously) we are activating the sympathetic nervous system. This isn't a bad thing in and of itself, it helps keep our airway expanded and all that jazz. But if we are out of our zone of tolerance, and want to encourage our parasympathetic response, changing our tongue position can speed up the process. Moving our tongue out of that position activates us going back into our ventral vagal window of tolerance.

If your tongue tends to get stuck and clenchy when activated, take a sip of water and hold it in your mouth, letting your tongue "float" in the water. Or stick your tongue in a glass of water to help detach it from your hard palate.

# The Felt Sense

One important way of working with our body-brain connection is to deepen our recognition of how our bodies react to stimuli. We learned some physiology basics in the last exercise, like about how our heart rate and skin color respond to different vagal states. Now we are going to get a little more nuanced.

The *felt sense* refers to the inner feelings of the body. It's also termed *interoception*. It includes things like noticing when your chest is tight or your stomach is rumbly.

The idea originates with Eugene Gendlin, who was a couples therapist in the 1950s who was trying to find the common thread in why some of his couples were able to achieve their goals and heal their relationships, and others ended up getting divorced. He couldn't find an obvious thread regarding the type of problem that brought them to counseling, so he started going through hundreds of hours of tapes of therapy sessions and had an aha moment after some time. The people who "got better" were the ones who were able to go quiet and still and listen to bodies rather than just stay in their brains and listen to their thoughts. He termed this the *felt sense,* and thought, "Well what if we teach people to do this?"

So he created a technique called *Focusing* and published a book by the same name in 1978. He has a six-part system, but has always maintained that anything that helps you get to the felt sense is totally awesome, which means that many tricks and tips have been formulated over the past decades. And as the connection between polyvagal theory and interoception become clearer more recently, felt sense work has become more common.

Here are several exercises designed to increase your internal full-body awareness. (And yes, the breathing and mindfulness exercises later on in this workbook are also very useful in this regard.)

## *INTEROCEPTION*

This exercise helps us feel into our bodies in a deliberate way, which can be helpful when we are either hypervigilant to external information or dissociating and shutting down. Learning to connect to our felt sense helps us develop a better working relationship with our vagus nerve, so we can recognize when we are out of our zone of tolerance and work to get back into it.

I use this exercise (adapted from Peter Levine's book *In An Unspoken Voice*) all the time with clients as a skill for managing trauma reactivity, internal overwhelm, and dissociation. Want to get an idea of where I'm going with this?

- Hold out one of your hands. It doesn't matter which one, but take note of your choice.

- Hold it in the air, without letting it rest against another surface (like a table top or your leg) for support. If you cannot comfortably do so, then absolutely use a surface for support.

- Open up the palm of that hand, facing back toward your body, and use your eyes to observe it.

- Slowly make a fist with that hand, watching the whole time. Take note when your hand feels completely closed into a fist.

- Without breaking eye contact, open your hand back up.

Now close your eyes if it feels safe for you to do so. If not, try softening your gaze so you aren't looking at anything in particular (instead of focusing on your hand) and repeat this exercise.

Feel what having your hand open feels like from the inside, then the act of closing your hand into a fist, then reopening. Pay attention to all that you notice in your body that wasn't present when you were focusing on your external sight messages.

How did your awareness of the experience change once you were entirely dependent on your internal sense messages? Was it disconcerting at any point? Comforting? Did anything shift or feel different in how you connect with yourself?

I have also had clients use their feet with the exercise, but making sure to keep them connected to the floor for grounding. Try flexing and wiggling your toes with and without visual stimulus and see if the experience changes for you any.

How did your awareness of this experience change once you were totally dependent on your internal sense messages?

Was it disconcerting at any point? Comforting?

Did anything shift or feel different in how you connect with yourself?

## P.A.T.H.

This is another interoception exercise, with the goal of connecting to the felt sense and recognizing your body's messaging. It adds some parameters to the sensory data you are paying attention to, which is helpful if your senses feel overwhelmed. This exercise is less for calming yourself when things are crap, and more for gaining more clarity over how your body communicates in all kinds of situations.

Turn your attention inward instead of the environment around you. Part of you will continue to pay attention to the environment to keep you safe, while you relax your body and soften your gaze but leave your eyes open.

Now, ask yourself the following four things about your body right now.

**P.** Where can I feel pressure?

**A.** Where can I feel the air around me on my body?

**T.** Where is there tension?

**H.** Where can I feel heat?

## FINDING THE WORDS

As you feel more comfortable in working with your felt sense you can expand your awareness of the sensations you are experiencing. Just like emotions, sensations are intended to give us information not to last forever.

Here is some sensory vocabulary:

Burning/Hot/Cold/Warm/Chilly/Icy/Cool/Clammy/Chilly/Sweaty/Gentle

Sharp/Dull/Rough/Smooth

Shaky/Trembly/Tingly/Twitchy/Butterflies/Jittery/Jumbled/Jangly/Itchy/
Jumpy

Weird/Off-Kilter/Off-Center/Edgy/Tearful/Owie

Hard/Soft

Stuck/Weak

Strong/Tough

Small/Large

Sour/Sweet/Bitter/Salty/Pungent

Relaxed/Calm/Peaceful/Flowing/Spreading/Silky/Still/Tranquil/Comfortable

Undisturbed/Chill/Still/Quiet/Peaceful Empty/Full Fast/Slow/Still

Tight/Tense/Pressure/Vibrating/ Dizzy/Fuzzy/Blurry/Woozy/Faint/Light-
Headed

Numb/Prickly/Tickly/Goose-Bumpy/Uncomfortable

Light/Heavy

Open/Closed/Loose/Tight

Some of the body sense words that may help you define your experience include:

Pressure, Air Current, Pain, Tingling, Itching, Temperature, Size, Weight, Shape,
Motion, Speed, Texture, Earth Element, Color, Smell, Taste, Sound, Lack of
Sensation

Because this is a pretty big list it may feel like writing a thesis on your body. Start by just noticing a couple of things. Maybe start with two or three opposite possibilities and decide which fits best. For example, does it feel tight or loose? Heavy or light?

It can also help to compare your feelings at different times. Practice by examining your current feelings, and then pick this book up in various other situations and see what changes you might notice when you're stressed, when you're unwinding, after different kinds of interactions, first thing in the morning, before bed, or whatever other situations you find yourself in..

Feelings I am experiencing *right now:*

Situation: _____

How I felt

Situation: _____

How I felt

## *SELF-HOLDING*

The goal of this exercise is to remember that our body is a container for our sensations and feelings. Dissociation sometimes leads to us not even realizing we have edges. A holding exercise helps us recognize our container, connect to it, and ground within it. It helps us "settle" even when experiencing uncomfortable emotions and sensations.

There are several ways to do this exercise. Here is a basic version, but keep in mind it can be done laying down, sitting up, or some kind of in-between reclining.

### Self-Hug

- Place one hand under the arm on the opposite side of your body, and the other hand over the upper part of the other arm.

- Give yourself a hug. The light squeezing can soothe the nervous system the same as getting under a heavy blanket.

- Now just pay attention to your body. Don't try to force any reactions but see what shifts within you.

What was your SUDS level before and after?

What did you notice in your body (much calmer, weird but helpful, just weird, etc.)

In what circumstances would this be of most benefit?

Are there any adjustments that would make it work even better for you?

## LISTENING TO YOUR BODY

Our subconscious is attending to far more incoming information than our conscious mind is. The study of information refers to this idea as *compression theory*. In a nutshell, we are taking in 11 million bits of data any given second, but can only consciously attend to about 50 of those bits in the same given second. Data compression (also called compaction) is the process of reducing the amount of information available. If we are compressing a bunch of computer files into a ZIP drive, that's *lossless*…meaning all the original data is still there. In the human brain, it is *lossy* (yes that's the real word), meaning that some information gets lost in the translation process.

The difference between zip drives and human brains is pretty important, right?

Physiologists were also the people to discover that we have a way of compensating for our human data compression process which lies in the body (which is why I got into hypnotherapy to begin with, it connects the entirety of the body with the working subconscious mind). It's our *reflex system,* which kicks in within 1/10th of a second of confronting stimulus. These are a lot of science-y terms to explain that we have a reaction with our bodies to what's going on around us, even if the information never gets processed on a conscious level.

At a subconscious level, our body is saying "oh, fuck no" to boundary violations in a very real way, through something called *visceral afferent messaging.* This just means an inward feeling from the body, telling the mind what to do, instead of the mind making a decision telling the body what to do. This information is relayed through the vagus nerve through something called *monoaminergic neurons* (and now you are super ready for bar trivia night!!).

TL;DR? *Gut reactions are real, literal things.*

And since the vagus nerve is involved, these body-based messages are signaling our whole system which is why you may notice things like a racing heart, feeling tearful, chills, difficulty breathing, and other physical markers of fear. Paying attention to the dude that lives in your stomach may save your life and can definitely save you some heartache.

How does your body warn you of danger? What do you notice?

Consider a situation where your gut instincts told you something and you ignored those instincts? What led you to ignore these instincts?

Do you have situations that may have caused faulty wiring regarding your gut instincts? An overactive danger response because of a trauma history? Or were you socially conditioned to *not* listen to your gut growing up?

If this is the case, who are your trusted people that you can check in with to verify if your gut instincts are on point or off-kilter?

## LEARNING YOUR BODY'S RESPONSES

This is a great exercise to try with another person (and can be done in a group training where everyone has a chance to process their experiences after). Touch can be involved (shaking hands, hugging, etc.) in this activity but doesn't have to be. Instead, you can try it with borrowing/using something that belongs to you, or getting closer in someone's space without actually touching.

The point is to practice learning how your body responds when you agree to something that you don't really want to do, and when you decline to do or disagree with something you really do want to do. It helps you discover your boundaries within your physical body by listening to the cues. Take note of your reactions and write them down below.

In this activity come up with things that you do want to do with the person you are practicing with...and don't want to do (but nothing awful or triggering... just something you wouldn't be thrilled with outside the parameters of this experiment, like letting them look through your bag or put their arm around your shoulder or something). Practice saying "yes" when you mean it as well as when you don't mean it. Then the same with "no." Notice what goes on in your body.

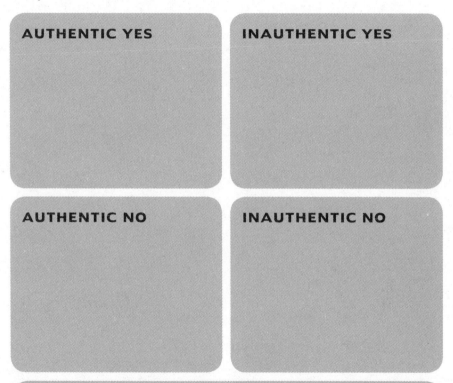

**AUTHENTIC YES**

**INAUTHENTIC YES**

**AUTHENTIC NO**

**INAUTHENTIC NO**

*Did you have any "I don't know/I'm not sure/Maybe/I feel confused" experiences? What did those feel like?*

# STRESS

We talk about stress and being stressed probably more regularly than we discuss any other aspect of our health and wellness. However, it has become so big and so vague that we lose sight of the fact that stress isn't external events. And we have far more control over our stress response than we do over our toxin exposure.

Stress is how our body responds to life events with the appropriate output of resources. Stress is heavily influenced by our life events (stressors), the chronic nature of them, and even our perceptions of them. And understanding all of this isn't as complicated as most research papers would have you believe and is a very important part of anyone's personal wellness plan.

Stress affects us all differently. Some people thrive on it and use that energy to get shit done. Others feel overwhelmed and check out. Maybe you get energized and motivated. Maybe your shoulders get tight. Maybe your whole body gets tight. Maybe you yell at people or drive recklessly. Maybe you space out. We all respond differently based on our previous experiences.

## Is It Stress or Anxiety?

The essential difference between anxiety and stress is whether the pressure we are feeling is internal or external. Anxiety comes from our own internal narrative about what we need to do, should do, are not doing, etc. And stress is the stuff coming into us from other people or events. Anxiety about job performance would be you not thinking you're doing enough, while stress would come from your boss telling you that you aren't doing enough. Of course, you can have stress and anxiety at once, but untangling them can help. Here is a space for you to map out the different internals and externals so you can tailor your approach as needed.

| Internal Anxieties | External Stressors |
| --- | --- |
| | |

Any connections between how the two columns reinforce each other?

## Stress Assessment

Consider your own history with stress:

What kinds of avoidant coping skills have you used in the past?

What other kinds of coping skills have you used that aren't avoidant of the stressor but are ultimately unhealthy for you?

What opportunities have you missed in an attempt to avoid the stress that would come along with them?

How might you be limiting your future?

# Reframing Stress

The author of the book *The Upside of Stress*, Kelly McGonigal, (whose research is the starting point for a lot of what I write about here) states: *"Embracing stress is a radical act of self trust."*

We've been told not to though, haven't we? We're told to avoid stress, to calm down, that it isn't good for us. Harvard Business School professor Alison Wood Brooks asked hundreds of people the same question: If you are anxious about a big presentation, what's a better way of handling it? Feeling excited or trying to calm down?

91% of people said "try to calm down."

But, as mentioned eleventy times above, the stress isn't in and of itself bad—it's not necessarily a problem you need to solve or get away from. This is borne out by multiple studies, including the one mentioned above, where the researchers found that just saying *"I'm excited"* out loud can reappraise stress as excitement. Despite what most of us have been told, it's easier for the brain to jump from anxious feelings to excited ones rather than calm ones. Cortisol is going to be activated because something matters to you. But you can consciously label it as excited instead of stressed, which changes how you interpret and experience your own body.

This is a form of mindset training. Chanting "I'm excited" or "I'm motivated" or "I'm in the zone" won't make objective stressors go away, but it can help you become more resilient, and also keep you from shutting down and saying no to things you want to do because everything seems so stressful.

Use the worksheet on the next page to make a list of what stresses you out. Then try to rephrase each thing to something you can legitimately feel excited about. Finally, remind yourself why you care enough to be stressed about the thing in the first place.

I am stressed about...

I am excited about...

This matters to me because...

# Having a **GOOD** Mindset

Mindset training has a direct impact on our stress response. One study found that a stronger physical stress response was associated with higher test scores in school situations, but only for people who have had mindset training. Another study demonstrated that just by telling people *"You're the kind of person whose performance improves under pressure"* increases their task performance by 33%. One of the biggest predictors of stress overwhelming us is our perception of not being up to the task, so focusing on the fact that we are, indeed, up to it shifts our thinking.

You can practice mindset training as part of your daily self-care routine. I like the GOOD acronym of mindset training since it doesn't involve any kind of fake hype about shitty situations, it really just is about being grounded in your own self-efficacy. And clearly you are a fucking survivor—you're reading this right now, which means your survival rate thus far is 100%, right?

This is one of those internal work exercises that might be easier to make external by journaling through it, especially at first while you get used to the process.

**Gratitude**: Focusing on gratitude is a really good part of our mental health in general and can create a perspective shift in our day. This doesn't mean discounting what's problematic, but focusing more on what's good in your life. Today I am grateful for:

**Openness to Possibilities**: If we are gratitude focused, we are far more likely to be aware of solutions, support, and opportunities around us. In a negative mindset, we are more likely to dismiss things that are available to us (or not notice them at all) because we are overwhelmed and frustrated with life in general.

Today I choose to be open to:

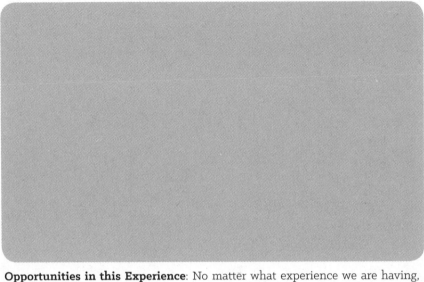

**Opportunities in this Experience**: No matter what experience we are having, we can focus on the opportunities that exist to help us grow. We can learn more about different situations and ourselves even if we don't achieve the success we were hoping for.

Today I recognize the opportunities to:

**Determine**: Visualize yourself successfully embracing the challenges ahead. This is hardiness in action. If you mentally set yourself up for success, you are in the right frame of mind to tackle the project. And no, you aren't more frustrated if things don't go perfectly.

Today success looks like:

## What Is in My Control?

Sometimes our anxiety, worries, and stress feel out of control because they elicit such strong reactions in our body . . . and because we are focused on the aspects of the situation that actually are outside of our control. Worrying about things we have no influence over gives our brains a false sense that we are doing something about them, rather than shifting our focus on the aspects of the situation where we do have some control. Stepping back and figuring out what has us stuck in an unproductive loop can help to get some clarity about what we can't do so that we can be free to focus on what we can do.

We're drawing a distinction here between control and influence—control means things that you have entire ownership of, whereas influence is stuff that you are likely to be able to impact by communicating and behaving as effectively as possible.

For your biggest anxiety or worry, break out your concerns and potential actions into three spheres.

My biggest concern:

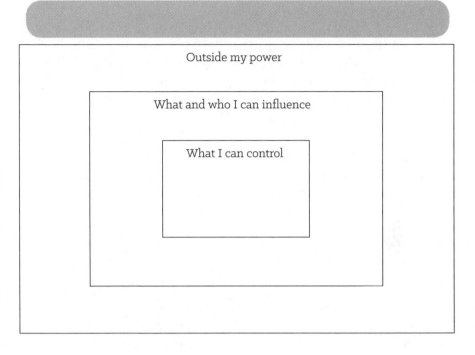

## Positive Thinking

Positive thinking sounds cheesy, but it works. This is different from being pollyanna-ish and pretending things are just fine when they are a shit-show. By contrast, positive thinking frames our experience around whatever control we do have in any given situation, who helps us activate our own ability to not just survive but thrive.

One proven method you can use to shift your thinking is journaling. There is so much research out there on journaling and how it affects mental health. Probably because it's a cheap thing to study. But also because it is an activity humans have engaged in since we developed the ability to read and write, which way predates the field of psychology.

Journaling has been found to be helpful with specific struggles with anxiety (trait anxiety) as well as with low-key continuous anxiety (state anxiety). It helps us manage stress and maintain a positive mood (read: window of tolerance).

One specific journal exercise designed to build a positive mindset has been shown to have a direct impact on vagal tone:

> Each day for three days in a row, reflect on a positive experience in your life, and imagine yourself back in that experience. Think about your emotions and how you felt in your body when it happened. Write about the experience in as much detail as possible, especially focusing on the thoughts, feelings, and sensations that went along with it.

Even better news? You only have to journal for three days to see results. Not thirty. Just three. We can all handle that. And if you are the student who is always going for extra credit, you can absolutely continue past day three.

## Four Ps

In my weird quest to make ideas easy to remember, I came up with this "4P" stress management protocol (is that a 5th P????). It's designed to be a mnemonic that condenses all the research on having a positive stress response into four steps you can use in your everyday life. Think about the next stressful situation you know you're going to encounter and go ahead and map it out here.

**PREP:** What's in my toolkit?

**PLAN:** How am I going to manage this situation, using the aforementioned toolkit?

**PROACT:** What is my process to activate this plan ahead of time?

**PERSEVERE:** How will I use this chemical energy to stay engaged?

## Stress After-Action Report

No matter what stress management plan you use, the important part is evaluating whether or not it was actually useful for you. Because we don't have time to continue doing dumb and unhelpful things, right? So let's unpack.

Stressful situation #1:

What did I handle well?

What did I learn that I will infuse into the future?

Stressful situation #2:

What did I handle well?

What did I learn that I will infuse into the future?

Stressful situation #3:

What did I handle well?

What did I learn that I will infuse into the future?

Stressful situation #4:

What did I handle well?

What did I learn that I will infuse into the future?

Stressful situation #5:

What did I handle well?

What did I learn that I will infuse into the future?

# BREATHWORK AND MINDFULLNESS

Our breath might be the most powerful tool we have to regulate our vagal system, expel toxins, heal from trauma, manage inflammation, and control stress. I know, that's some gross-ass hippie shit. I'm sorry. But it's true. And bonus points that it's free. You're doing it anyway, so doing it somewhat differently can end up being world changing for you.

Breath (*pranayama*), along with the topics of the next two chapters which are meditation (*dhyana*) and movement (the *asanas*), just happen to be three of the eight limbs of yoga. Now, I super pinky-swear I am not trying to trick you into doing yoga if that's not your jam, but when I was framing out this book it became pretty obvious pretty quickly that Patanjali figured out in the 2nd Century BCE, way before "modern" science did, that these are good ways to keep your body and mind healthy and connected to each other.

Breathing is also a super-important component of mindfulness and meditation, it is the universally present anchor that we can use to stay embodied in the present.

Mindfulness is the basic human ability to be aware and fully present in our own lives, to bear witness to the workings of our body and mind as well as what is going on around us. John Kabat-Zinn, likely the best known mindfulness instructor in the Western world, states that mindfulness is just *awareness*. It is the natural state of the human body, especially when we are young, but it is something we become trained out of when we developmentally get to the place where we realize we can escape our present reality and be somewhere else. In fact, we do that so often researchers have found that at least half of our waking hours are spent with wandering minds.

Mindfulness does not require meditation. Mindfulness is essentially the best path we have figured out for accepting the is-ness of our lives. This isn't to say that we should take shit lying down, it's about recognizing the reality of the current moment rather than getting so wrapped up into how we want it to be/how it should be that we get stuck. When we get stuck in how things should be we get stuck in unceasing judgement, which is not a place systemic change comes from.

Meditation, by contrast, is a formal process of focused attention and does not have to include mindfulness. For instance, a mantra meditation is creating a new present moment with a specific repeated sound while mindfulness meditation is just about being in the present moment.

Mindfulness meditation is where the two meet. This is where that process of awareness is brought into the formal practice of focused attention. This doesn't mean perfect attention, but it is a process of recognizing when the mind wanders and refocusing awareness back to the present when it does, usually with some kind of anchor (the breath is the most common).

There is not a "correct" form of mindfulness, meditation, or mindfulness meditation. They all have the same goal of helping achieve a peaceful mind and manage stress so I am including a wide variety of practices for you to experiment with in this chapter.

Doing breathwork and mindfulness are a good time to practice interoception. Thich Nhat Hanh says that once we start practicing nontalking and nonthinking, we actually make space to listen to ourselves. All of the fears and pains that we have shoved down can now come forward and be cared for by us. So as you're doing these exercises, pay attention to what you feel inside your body, where you feel it, and how strongly. I've provided a log at the end of this chapter to track your feelings and responses in each exercise. You can use the list of physical sensations words on page 74.

Some of these exercises come with contraindications. Just like something being a whole food supplement or herb doesn't make it a good choice for your body and circumstances, some breathing techniques may also be a bad idea. But hey, other than that?

# A Note about Trauma

Like any other intervention, those of us with trauma histories may need to take an extra special approach to breathwork, meditation, and mindfulness.

I have over a decade of formal meditation practice and a pretty intense amount of clinical training in both breathwork and mindfulness. It can be (it *is*) still really difficult. I know. *I know.* Conscious alteration of your breathing when you are triggered or activated may feel completely undoable. Someone *telling* you how to do it feels even worse. Likewise, sitting down to meditate may provide an opportunity for all sorts of thoughts and feelings and memories to rush in that you may not have been prepared for. So if you have had an awful experience in a meditation class or a yoga class, with a therapist, or listening to an app, you aren't the least bit crazy, that's really common. So I want to talk a little about why that is and how to plan for it.

Trauma changes our breathing. When we are out of our zone of tolerance, our breathing becomes shallow (to change oxygen movement throughout the body to prepare for the perceived attack). And trauma survivors often hold their breath regularly without realizing it. And that creates tension and more body dysregulation that we are often even aware of.

We can learn from yoga practitioners like David Emerson who have been developing trauma-informed practices that can help you use mindful movement and breathing for trauma recovery, without being retraumatized or triggered by it. David Emerson's trauma-informed yoga is an evidence-based practice for trauma recovery, and there are several unique aspects to how he cues yoga that I use as a teacher and clinician.

One of the biggest differences in his approach is that he doesn't tell practitioners when to breathe in and out. He only suggests noticing it. If you have taken a more traditional yoga class, you'll remember being told when to breathe in and breathe out constantly. By contrast, the first breathwork exercise in this chapter is designed to help you just *notice* your breath, with no plan of altering it. Trauma survivors regularly struggle to notice their breathing at all, so beginning to do so is a really big deal. And it helps us notice when we are holding our breath as well. While an anxiety or panic response can include very rapid, shallow breathing, a trauma response may invoke a locked jaw, breath suppression, and abdominal inhibition.

Having a trauma history, or having a trauma response while meditating or doing breathwork, doesn't mean you can't do these exercises. But those of us with intense trauma histories need to have space for *choice*. This means choice in working through a trauma history in our own time and in our own way, instead of having memories flood our present moment and disrupt our lives. Traditional meditation practices encourage us to go back to the breath and to treat any triggers or activation as thinking that detracts from the present moment. Instead, a trauma informed practice helps us lean into uncomfortable feelings without losing our zone of tolerance.

If trauma is an issue for you, here are some tips, many of them inspired by David Treleaven's book *Trauma-Sensitive Mindfulness*.

- Recognize your internal *go* and *stop* signals (thoughts, feelings, body sensations) as markers of how you respond to different techniques. Which are most helpful? Which are activating?

- You don't have to be in physical pain either. Take breaks when you need to or alter how you are holding your body. Move into a more comfortable position or wiggle in place a little.

- Open your eyes, if they have been closed. If you want to work up to practicing with your eyes closed, start with a soft gaze.

- Change to slow, mindful breathing if you were trying one of the more complicated pranayama techniques.

- Focus on an external object that is in your line of vision.

- Shorten your breathwork practice period or otherwise adjust the practice itself (for example, the 4-7-8 breathing pattern can be altered to shorter breaths).

- If your practice involves attending a class, talk to the teacher first. If it's a movement clas, you can ask them not to touch you to make adjustments.

Learn and practice breathwork and meditation when you are in a relaxed state, rather than trying to do it when you are already activated. The more you practice when your body isn't under siege, the more likely you are to be successful with it when your body *is* under siege.

# Noticing the Breath

*No specific contraindications.*

Settle your body into a comfortable position. You can close your eyes if you feel comfortable doing so, or settle into a soft gaze instead.

Bring your awareness to your breathing. Notice as you breathe in, and follow through as you breathe out. When your thoughts wander, just notice them, maybe label them as thinking, and bring your attention back to the breath. You can use Thich Naht Hahn's breathing mindfulness technique to help center your focus on being mindful in the moment:

> *Breathing in, I know I am breathing in...*
>
> *Breathing out, I know I am breathing out.*
>
>
> *Breathing in... I know I am breathing in...*
>
> *Breathing out... I know I am breathing out...*

Notice the rhythm of your breathing, notice how it changes. Notice the sensations in the rest of your body and how they change. Don't do anything to alter your breathing or to "breathe better," just pay attention to where you are now.

You can use whatever words work for you to focus you on your breathing:

*Breathing in.....*

*Breathing out.....*

# Three-part Breathing

*No specific contraindications.*

We've all done a big inhale before starting a new task, right? The inhale is our sympathetic nervous system becoming activated, which gives us an energy boost to act. Someone in distress is breathing so rapidly they are constantly inhaling, building up an energy flow that tells the brain to become anxious or panic.

The exhale is the parasympathetic response, which lowers our heart rate and calms our energy.

The retention (the space between inhale and exhale) is the space where we connect with our body and what's going on inside it (interoception). So the 4-7-8 breathing pattern is designed to manage a stress response by lengthening out our periods of interoception and parasympathetic engagement.

- Breathe in for a count of 4

- Hold for a count of 7

- And out for a count of 8

You may feel a little light headed at first, and it's totally okay to sit or lie down. Another option is to use the same ratio, but shorten it:

- Breathe in for a count of 2

- Hold for a count of 3.5

- And out for a count of 4

# The Complete Breath (Dirgha Pranayama)

*Don't do Dirgha if you've had recent abdominal surgery, or if you have throat or sinus irritation or a respiratory infection.*

Dirgha is a good daily practice to help manage breathing errors that we have collected over time. While you don't (and really can't) breathe like this 24/7, practicing with it daily will help you naturally lengthen and deepen and relax your "regular" breathing naturally.

- Get in a comfortable position—seated is best for this practice. Hold your spine as straight as you are comfortably able to, and let your abdomen soften.

- Place your hands on your abdomen or bring awareness to that area. Gradually start to lengthen and deepen your breathing. Work to expand your belly like a balloon with each inhale, and deflate it back out upon exhale. This is abdominal (or belly breathing).

- Now shift your attention to your ribcage. If you are able to place your hands on the side of your ribcage, do so and focus your breathing into that space. Feel the flexibility of your ribs as you expand them on inhale and relax them on exhale.

- Now shift your attention to your upper chest. If you are able to, place the tips of your fingers on the front of your chest right below the collar bone. Focus breathing into this area, bringing awareness to your chest lifting slightly upon inhale, and softening back into your body on exhale.

- Try combining all three parts. Exhale fully, then focus on inhaling into the belly, up through ribcage, and then through the upper lungs. Gradually release the breath, noticing how the upper lungs, rib cage, and belly deflate as you do so.

## Alternate Nostril Exercise (Nadi Shodhana Pranayama)

*Don't do alternate breathing if you have hypertension, an active migraine, or an active sinus or chest infection. Also generally be aware of discomfort if you have a full stomach.*

This technique is great for balancing the left and right hemispheres of the brain and balancing the vagal system. Studies of pranayama have demonstrated that alternate nostril breathing was the only type of breath work that was found to have a positive effect on the cardiovascular system (heart rate, respiratory rate, and blood pressure).

This breathing exercise involves breathing from alternate nostrils. This exercise cleans nostrils and sinuses. It is also helpful in the activation left and right side of the brain simultaneously.

- Get your body comfortable, sitting if possible.

- Place your left hand on your left knee, and lift your right hand up to your nose.

- Tuck your middle three fingers into the palm of your hand, leaving your pinky and thumb extended (the universal sign for "call me!")

- Complete an exhale, then use your right thumb to close your right nostril. Inhale through your left nostril.

- Use your pinky to close your left nostril while opening your right nostril and exhaling through the right nostril.

- That is one complete breath cycle. Continue for up to five minutes, making sure that you always finish your practice by finishing with an exhale on the left side.

## Bee Breath (Bhramari Pranayama)

*Don't do bee breath if you are actively suffering a migraine. Also generally be aware of discomfort if you have a full stomach.*

This technique has been shown to reduce stress and anger, help with sleep induction, and helps strengthen the muscles of the throat.

- Get comfortable, sitting upright if possible.

- Take a full inhalation

- Hold for three seconds,

- Close your ears using your index fingers

- Make a soft humming sound on exhale (like the sound of a buzzing honeybee).

- Repeat 5-6 times if possible.

As an alternative to closing your ears, you can place your thumb on the cartilage between your cheeks and your ears, so you feel the vibration but aren't blocking off your hearing.

# Ocean Sounding Breath (Ujjaji Breathing)

*No specific contraindications.*

This technique is fantastic for centering and focusing concentration without the nervous system activation that usually comes along with increasing our attention.

- Sit comfortably, upright if possible.

- Relax your jaw and keep your lips closed.

- Start with some deep breathing to bring your body's focus back to breathwork.

- Now softly contract the back of your throat so you are making a "hhhhhhhh" sound upon inhale and exhale. Think of how you would use your throat to fog up a mirror. It can also be helpful to hold your cupped hands in front of your mouth and breathe into them so it sounds like holding a seashell up to your ear.

If it's hard to hear yourself, some people do well using headphones to block out other noise so they can hear the sound from inside their head. It's much easier to create the ocean sounding breath on exhale than inhale, so focus on exhale first if you are practicing this technique and it's taking you awhile to get it down.

# Breathwork Log

Here's a place to keep track of the breathwork techniques you are trying and their effectiveness. Keeping track like this is especially helpful when your brain wants to act super hopeless about everything and you need a reminder that you are making good progress and not wasting your time.

| Technique | SUDs before | SUDs after | How I felt |
|-----------|-------------|------------|------------|
|           |             |            |            |

# Basic Mindfulness Meditation Instructions

This is the classic, go-to mindfulness based meditation that uses breath as the anchor to the present moment.

- Settle in a comfortable position. Sitting with an aligned back is the classic method (either on a cushion or in a straight backed chair) but if that isn't a position you can get into or maintain, no worries—settle your body to be as presence-focused as possible.

- Bring your awareness to the physical sensations of your body. Where do you feel the pressure of your body making contact with your chair, bed, or floor? What other sensations (like air, temperature, texture) do you notice? Spend a minute or two noticing those sensations.

- Now bring your awareness to your lower abdomen, recognizing the sensations of your breath moving in and out of your body. You can place a hand on your abdomen to help you feel the sensation if you are struggling to make that connection if that's helpful. Notice your abdominal wall stretching and inflating with each in-breath and gently deflating with each out breath.

- Continue to follow the breath in and out, giving yourself permission to just be in the experience of your breath.

- Eventually (probably sooner rather than later) you will notice that your mind is wandering. You start daydreaming, planning, getting consumed with other thoughts. My brain likes to sing songs and make shopping lists, personally. This is what brains do. It doesn't make you a mindful meditation failure. Just when you notice that you're doing it, label it "thinking" and focus back on the breath.

- Bring curiosity and patience to your wanderings, rather than frustration. Notice what was going on and return to the breath.

Most research demonstrates that 15 minutes of practice is the amount of time it takes to gain the benefits of mindfulness meditation. If you can't tolerate it for that long, that's also okay. Practice working up to it. If you find that it's helpful and want to extend time out further that's also great, but not required.

# Mindfully Eating a Raisin

This mindful eating practice is a classic MBSR (mindfulness-based stress reduction) technique. It gives you a different element to focus on, other than your breath.

- Place a few raisins in your hand. And no you don't have to use raisins, any food will do. I've found that even people who don't like raisins are not bothered by them in this exercise. But if they really gross you out, grab something else.

- Pretend this is your first day on the planet. This is a new food that you have never seen before, and you are an alien explorer that is going to make scientific study of raisins and raisin-ness. Use all five of your senses to explore it. Turn it around with your fingers, notice the color, the tactical sensations. How does it fold or reflect light? What does it smell like when you hold it up to your nose? Does it make any sound if you apply pressure?

- You will start having thoughts of the "Why am I doing this? This is fucking weird" variety. Totally normal. Just recognize them as a thought you are having and bring yourself back to the activity.

- Bring the object slowly to your mouth. Notice how automatic it is for your hand to bring nourishment up to your mouth. Notice whatever anticipation you are experiencing. Is your mouth watering? Gently place the raisin on your tongue without biting down. Explore the sensation of the raisin in your mouth.

- When you are ready, bite down. Notice the taste that is released when doing so. Notice how you habitually move it to one side of your mouth over another. Slowly chew the raisin. Notice how it changes in texture, and flavor as you chew. When you feel ready to swallow, notice your conscious intention to do so. Pay attention to the sensation of it moving down your throat, to your esophagus.

How did the experience of eating differ when you did so mindfully? What did you notice? What did you enjoy? What was uncomfortable?

You can try this exercise with any type of food or beverage. Track your experiments below and see what works for you.

Food: _____

Experience

Food: _____

Experience

Food: _____

Experience

Food: _____

Experience

# Metta Meditation

Metta loosely translates *loving-kindness*. In essence, it's a focus of general goodwill, friendliness, and open-heartedness. It's a way of engaging in the world without all shields up, feeling defensive and ill at ease.

A metta meditation involves focusing not just on the breath, but on a series of healing statements about yourself, another person or group of people, or the world.

The original texts from the Buddha on metta (as translated from *The Discourse on Loving-Kindness*) is:

> *Wishing: In gladness and in safety, may all beings be at ease.*
>
> *Whatever living beings there may be, omitting none*
>
> *Let none deceive another, or despise any being in any state*
>
> *Let none through anger or ill will wish harm upon another.*

These statements have an archaic language (and don't worry, we're gonna use a more modern format), but speak to universal human struggles across time. Specifically, the harm we experience just by being a human living in an imperfect world, and the continued harm (suffering) that we impose on ourselves in the process. Metta meditation allows us to work with the feelings we avoid the most, like aversion and despair. The Buddha stated that by working with uncomfortable emotions, we can transform them into something that serves us better.

When we don't like someone, doing a metta meditation on their behalf feels gross. My meditation instructor encourages focusing on the easiest people first, the people or living things we love and adore (yes, it can absolutely be your pup or your favorite tree in the park if you aren't feeling particularly people-y). After that, we can move to the people who are a little more sketch, and finally to the people we consider the most difficult as we build tools to release what about them creates toxic emotions within us.

Also, we should offer metta to ourselves. Self-hatred is far more common than hatred of others. Buddhist meditation instructor Sharon Salzberg discusses how this is a super common in Western culture as an offset of systemic oppression (defined by bell hooks as "imperialist white supremacist capitalist patriarchy"). Because no matter what set of circumstances or privileges we have accessed, no one measures up to these standards. We all struggle with not-enoughness and feel a continuous need to earn our space in the world, rather than recognizing that we deserve by the sheer fact that we are human.

Here are some more modernized metta meditation statements that you can use in your own practice, that are used more often now than the Buddha's originals. You can say these out loud or think them in your head, timed with your breath. Where there is a blank you insert "I" or "my" for doing metta for yourself, "you" or the name of the person you are focusing on, or "all" meaning the entirety of sentient beings.

- May _____ be protected and safe from harm from others

- May _____ be protected and safe from self-inflicted harm

- May _____ be happy

- May _____'s body support the practice of loving awareness

- May _____ be free from anxiety

- May _____ be free from anger

- May _____ be free from fear

- May _____ love themself/themselves exact as they are

- May _____ be free from suffering

- May _____ find peace in the world

- May _____ find balance between attachment and apathy

# Mantra Meditation

Using a mantra to meditate is the best known form of meditation that isn't mindfulness based. In Sanskrit, *man* translates to "mind," and *tra* means "to free from." Mantras are used as a tool to free the mind (or to be freed from the mind). They help break the cycle of spinning thoughts that lead to anxiety, self-doubt and the like. Transcendental Meditation, which relies on mantras, got really big when Maharishi Mahesh Yogi brought the ancient technique to the US.

As with other practices that have spiritual roots, researchers in the US were interested in how the techniques themselves, outside a cultural context, can alter physical and mentals states. Since the 1970s, Herbert Benson, professor of medicine at Harvard Medical School and founder of the Benson-Henry Institute for Mind Body Medicine at Massachusetts General Hospital, has studied what creates that meditative state, which he termed "the relaxation response" (with a bestselling book by the same name).

Benson has experimented with subjects repeating Sanskrit mantras as well as nonreligious words, such as "one." He's found that regardless of what the practitioner repeats, the word or phrase has nearly the same effects: relaxation and the ability to better cope with life's unexpected stressors. Mantras actually soothe the default mode of the brain,

keeping it from going into storytelling mode creating anxious thoughts.

Sanskrit chanting is often part of many practices, including different branches of yoga. The sanskrit often has complex meanings beyond the literal translations. I've found that learning the relevance and meaning behind mantras like *om mani padme hum* lends depth to my practice. But, mantras in any language have the same effect. You can chant any contemplative expression from your faith system (like "Hail Mary, full of grace") or something more generally spiritual (like "I am Divine Love"), or any secular humanist phrase, and gain the same default mode benefit. Or maybe there is a certain mantra about your path of healing that you want to use.

Once you've decided on a mantra, find your comfy place and set a timer for yourself. Start with a few deep breaths and then start changing your mantra (in your head is fine, outloud voice is also fine). If you catch your thoughts wandering, bring them back to the mantra.

Mantras to try:

# Meditation in Motion

What we often refer to as "walking meditation" is really just "meditation in motion." Whatever device you may use for mobility will become part of the process.

- Find an unobstructed space in which you can move back and forth in a reasonably straight line for about ten feet (yes, you can also do a greater distance). If you are walking and are able to do so barefoot (and it's an area that is safe for you to be barefoot), you may find it helpful to gain more awareness of how your body creates balance for movement.

- If you are walking, bring your attention to your feet, shifting your weight from side to side and front to back, as far as you are able to do so comfortably. Lift your head and chest so you are facing forward, let your shoulders drop away from your ears. You can clasp your hands behind your back, hold them in front of you, or let them hang loosely at your side.

- Lift up one of your legs. It doesn't matter which, but take notice. Pay attention to how your weight shifts in your body when you do so. What does the other side of your body need to do to hold your full weight. Move your lifted foot forward, then place your heel on the ground and roll the rest of your foot down, ending with your toes. Pay attention to how your other foot begins to lift and move forward as well. Bring that foot forward and repeat.

- If you use a device for mobility, focus your attention on the sensations of movement. Connect the sensation of using your hands to connect to the mobility support and guide you forward. Feel the sensation of moving forward and your connection of being embodied and supported in that experience. If you are using a chair that relies on voice, facial expression identification, or the like, focus on how you engage your body and connect to the chair to create movement. What shifts do you feel physically and energetically?

- No matter how you create movement, your mind will wander as minds like to do. As your attention wanders off, you can bring yourself back to present practice with the thought of "attention engagement forward" or an anchoring reminder of your choice.

- When you come to the end of your path (unless it was a circle to begin with), turn fully around, face the direction from which you came, and start over. If you are moving in a circular shape, simply notice that you have completed one full round.

## Meditation on the Soles of the Feet

This particular practice has been shown to be really beneficial for the management of aggression and anger.

- If you are standing, stand in whatever relaxed posture is most natural for you.

- If you are sitting, sit comfortably with the soles of your feet flat on the floor or another surface.

- Breathe normally. You don't have to do deep belly breaths or anything outside of how you regularly breathe.

- Now, think back on an incident that made you very angry. Stay with that anger. Let the angry thoughts flow through your mind without trying to stop them. You may notice your heart rate or breathing go up as you remember that anger.

- Now, shift all your attention to the soles of your feet.

- Slowly, move your toes, feel your shoes covering your feet, feel the texture of your socks or hose, the curve of your arch, and the heels of your feet against the back of your shoes. If you do not have shoes on, feel the floor or carpet with the soles of your feet.

- Keep breathing naturally and focus on the soles of your feet until you feel calm and the physical signs of anger dissipate, this will take probably 10 to 15 minutes.

- Slowly come out of your meditation, sit quietly for a few moments, and then resume your daily activities.

# Cognitive Defusion

Remember earlier when I talked about how we can practice mindfulness without doing so in the form of meditation? And how some forms of therapy aren't mindfulness-based but still center mindfulness as a core skill? Cognitive defusion is a technique from Acceptance and Commitment Therapy (ACT) that focuses on mindfulness in managing being overwhelmed without having to sit on a cushion with it. As with the other practices listed here, this is one I use with clients regularly.

This skill is designed to help manage thoughts that are painful, overwhelming, unkind, or unhelpful. We tend to over identify (fuse with) with our thoughts, so thinking something like "I'm terrible" or "I don't deserve love" can become the truths we operate within unless we approach them with mindfulness.

- Start by identifying a hurtful self-criticism that you want to work with. If you can shorten it into a phrase or single sentence, it's easier to work with than a rambling paragraph of self-recrimination (which is my personal speciality).

- Let yourself engage with the thought rather than try to push it away. You can repeat it to yourself mentally or verbalize it out loud.

- Now add this modifier in front of it: "I'm having the thought that…" so "I don't deserve love" becomes "I'm having the thought that I don't deserve love."

- Now take another step away from it by adding "I notice…" so we are now at "I notice I'm having the thought that I don't deserve love."

- It may be wordy and complex at first, but with some practice you may be able to shorten it into a sentence that really gets at the heart of the issue.

- Now reflect on whatever mental shifts you notice as you defused the thought by recognizing it as an experience your brain was having instead of your life operating instructions. What did you notice?

# Mindfulness Practice Log

Here's a place to keep track of any mindfulness, meditation, movement, or relaxation techniques you try.

| Technique | SUDs before | SUDs after | How I felt |
|-----------|-------------|------------|------------|
|  |  |  |  |

# UNFUCK YOUR MOVEMENT

**P**hysical exercise is good for us, and not because of burning calories, or how it might make our bodies look. But the idea of exercise often has a punitive connotation. Even the most benign definition of exercise I could find ("a subset of physical activity used for the specific purpose of promoting fitness and overall health") still reads as a chore to be completed, like: get your teeth cleaned, bring the dog to the groomer, and jump on the treadmill. Even if you like the results, the task itself being a chore is exactly the problem.

I'd like to change that. I'd like to reclaim moving our bodies because our bodies like to move. I want the process to be as joyful as the end result.

And I want to bring that sense of play back, in whatever way that makes sense to *you*. I happen to adore hiking, swimming, and yoga. And when I say yoga, I don't mean the sweaty kind that smells like feet and butts, but gentle practices. You may not like any of those things but maybe you adore basketball. Or gardening. Or maybe you are one of those people who digs running even when no one is chasing them with an axe. Or you used to. I want to encourage you to find that joy again. Or if you never had it, I hope that you can in some way find it.

I don't have a lot of fancy worksheets for you here, and I sure as hell am not going to ask you to count reps or log miles or whatever. Your task here is just getting out there and moving your body. But maybe taking notes on what feels good to your body will help motivate you to do that.

# Exercise Research

And I don't mean research about the calories you'll burn! Maybe you don't even know what kind of movement you want to try! That's okay. Here's some space to figure out what you might want to do and the logistics of getting out there to see if you actually enjoy it. Whether you want to join a kickball team, take a tai chi class at the gym, or go for a bike ride by the river, get your concrete next steps down here. That may mean requesting a schedule change at work or bribing a friend to attend with you. Anything pragmatic that gets you out exploring.

| Movement Idea | Class, Group, or Place near me | Next step |
|---|---|---|
| | | |

# Movement Log

Here you get to keep track of any movement you do and how it makes you feel!
The exertion part is not about reshaping your body but about figuring out how
you like to be embodied. Some people adore high intensity stuff, others hate it,
and you may not know where you fall on that spectrum or in different situations.

| Date | Movement | Duration | Exertion 1-10 | How I felt during | How I felt after | Notes |
|------|----------|----------|---------------|-------------------|------------------|-------|
|      |          |          |               |                   |                  |       |
|      |          |          |               |                   |                  |       |
|      |          |          |               |                   |                  |       |

# Mind Body Benefits Check-in: Movement

As you tracked stuff and made changes, what benefits did you notice? Track what makes sense to you, and feel free to add your own.

| Benefits | Better | The Same | Worse | How So? |
|---|---|---|---|---|
| Energy | | | | |
| Mental alertness | | | | |
| Emotional equanimity | | | | |
| Sleep quality | | | | |
| Pain | | | | |
| Headaches | | | | |
| Allergies | | | | |
| Asthma/ Breathing issues | | | | |
| General Illness | | | | |
| Sex stuff | | | | |
| PMS symptoms | | | | |
| Stress levels | | | | |
| Stress management | | | | |
| Chronic symptom flares | | | | |
| Blood sugar stability | | | | |
| Blood pressure | | | | |
| | | | | |
| | | | | |
| | | | | |
| | | | | |
| | | | | |

# UNFUCK YOUR SLEEP

S leep is the brain's own meditative state that happens about 8 hours out of every 24 (if we are doing it right) in accord with our circadian rhythm. During sleep, some parts of the brain become way less active and other parts of the brain become way more active.

Sleep is super important for all sorts of reasons, not least because it's when our bodies and brains flush out toxins, reduce chronic inflammation, support healing in both physical and emotiona domains.We have a culture of sleep deprivation, but operating under sleep deprivation doesn't mean you need less sleep than the average bear. I have lots of yelling about this in *Unfuck Your Body* packed with information and techniques that go way beyond the usual "drink less caffeine and have a bedtime routine" stuff (though yes, do those things). Here's we're just going to provide a place to keep track of your sleep habits, because that's another thing that helps. This will help you figure out what stuff is actually helping (whether it be different sleep meds or edibles or blue light blockers) so you can build your personalized sleep routine.

## Sleep Log

Knowledge is power! By keeping track of your sleep habits there's a lot you can learn about what you need to get better sleep. There are plenty of smartphone apps that will help you keep track of the duration and quality of your sleep, using your mic to pay attention to your breathing and movement, and I am a believer in using them. You can get even more granular by using this log, whether or not you use an app as well.

| NIGHT | Monday | Tuesday | Wednesday |
|---|---|---|---|
| Bedtime | | | |
| Wake-up time | | | |
| Hours asleep | | | |
| Times woke in night and why | | | |
| Nightmares | | | |
| Snoring/ breathing issues? | | | |
| Sleep quality (1-10) | | | |
| How it felt to wake up | | | |
| DAY | | | |
| Naps | | | |
| Exercise | | | |
| Energy | | | |
| Emotions | | | |
| Time of last caffeine | | | |
| Time of last alcohol | | | |
| Time of last food | | | |
| Time of last screen time without blue blockers | | | |
| Sleeping meds / supplements / aids taken | | | |

| Thursday | Friday | Saturday | Sunday |
| --- | --- | --- | --- |
| | | | |
| | | | |
| | | | |
| | | | |
| | | | |
| | | | |
| | | | |
| | | | |
| | | | |
| | | | |
| | | | |
| | | | |
| | | | |
| | | | |
| | | | |
| | | | |
| | | | |
| | | | |

# Mind Body Benefits Check-in: Sleep

| Benefits | Better | The Same | Worse | How So? |
|---|---|---|---|---|
| Energy | | | | |
| Mental alertness | | | | |
| Emotional equanimity | | | | |
| Sleep quality | | | | |
| Pain | | | | |
| Headaches | | | | |
| Allergies | | | | |
| Asthma/ Breathing issues | | | | |
| General Illness | | | | |
| Sex stuff | | | | |
| PMS symptoms | | | | |
| Stress levels | | | | |
| Stress management | | | | |
| Chronic symptom flares | | | | |
| Blood sugar stability | | | | |
| Blood pressure | | | | |
| | | | | |
| | | | | |
| | | | | |
| | | | | |
| | | | | |
| | | | | |

# UNFUCK YOUR EATING

**F**irst off, this part is not about dieting, counting calories, weight loss, BMIs, or any of that bullshit. I've got to say that one more time in case you missed it earlier because it's an important soap box for me. If you want to read my ranting on the subject, there's a lot of it in *Unfuck Your Body*, with all the science and history of why so much of the industry is based on trash "science." As well as some choice science and history about our food system and what sort of unhealthy food is widely available to us.

There is also the reality (also discussed in the book) that we have way more allergies and food intolerances than we used to. Our food system is incredibly ungreat. And our bodies suffer the consequences of what a handful of billionaires have created, prompted, and sustained. So figuring out how to better navigate a broken system is where this part of the workbook comes in.

A lot of times we may find that our physical ailments, from arthritis to low energy to weird rashes are a result of something we are so used to eating we just don't think of it. Often removing certain foods from our diet can make us feel a lot better and save us a lot of other issues both in the present and down the road.

I'm also providing some tools to help research ingredients because knowing what you're putting in your body is a good way to avoid putting a lot of toxic stuff in it. And there's also a worksheet to help figure out where to get local food.

# Elimination Diet Log

Before we start, if you have a history of restricting a variety of foods because of disordered eating and dieting, don't take this on. Getting a little bloated from tomatoes now and then is a small price to pay to keep from losing all of your recovery work. For everyone else, an elimination diet can be incredibly helpful if you are trying to parse out which foods are consistently making you feel like shit so you can make informed choices around their consumption.

Taking the time to figure out how your body best functions in regards to food can go a long way to helping your physical and mental health. The standard way to figure out if you have an allergy or sensitivity is through an elimination diet like Whole30, a low FODMAP diet, or the autoimmune protocol diet. If you think a particular type of food might be causing you problems, you can try eliminating the suspect alone but it can be more than one thing and/or a cascade effect. If you are suspicious that you have some food sensitivities, but aren't sure where to start, the most common allergens make the most sense, and are also the list of the most delicious stuff, for which I apologize in advance: milk, eggs, peanuts, soy, wheat, tree nuts, fish, and shellfish.

Elimination diets aren't meant to be long term. You generally only need to follow a restricted diet for about a month tops to give your body a chance to get rid of all traces of the possible offenders. And many people get really good benefits from a 10 day detox if 30 feels overwhelming. After dumping out the possible offenders for your set number of days you add one food back in every couple of days to see how your body responds and which ones end up getting shown the door with the message "and *stay* out!" You can use this worksheet to help keep track of what foods you reintroduce and what symptoms you experience. Symptoms to look for may include headache, bloating, rashes, stomach cramps, joint pain, fatigue, brain fog, etc.

What food or foods will you eliminate (or if you're trying one of the more intensive elimination diets, plan what you will continue eating during that period):

Length of elimination period: _____

First reintroduction date: _____

First reintroduction food: _____

What I ate: _____

Now return to the full elimination diet for two days.

Symptoms experienced during and after first reintroduction:

My verdict on the first reintroduction food:

Second reintroduction date: _____  _____

Second reintroduction food: _____

What I ate: _____

Now return to the full elimination diet for two days.

Symptoms experienced during and after second reintroduction:

My verdict on the second reintroduction food:

# Mind Body Benefits Check-in: Eating

| Benefits | Better | The Same | Worse | How So? |
|---|---|---|---|---|
| Energy | | | | |
| Mental alertness | | | | |
| Emotional equanimity | | | | |
| Sleep quality | | | | |
| Pain | | | | |
| Headaches | | | | |
| Allergies | | | | |
| Asthma/ Breathing issues | | | | |
| General Illness | | | | |
| Sex stuff | | | | |
| PMS symptoms | | | | |
| Stress levels | | | | |
| Stress management | | | | |
| Chronic symptom flares | | | | |
| Blood sugar stability | | | | |
| Blood pressure | | | | |
| | | | | |
| | | | | |
| | | | | |
| | | | | |
| | | | | |
| | | | | |

# Finding The Good Stuff

Eating whole, healthy foods that reduce your toxic load and are also delicious may require some research, which for me at least, activates a lot of overwhelm. Here are resources to get you started, and space to take notes about what you find.

## *INGREDIENTS RESEARCH*

EWG's *Healthy Living* app lets you scan  both food and personal care product information to help you inform choices

The *Is It Vegan?* app allows you to scan products to see if they are plant-based or not. This can be useful even if you aren't vegan but are avoiding eggs, dairy, certain types of meat, etc.

There are tons of apps and databases that focus on sustainability (like the *Monterey Bay Aquarium Seafood Watch* app) and reducing food waste in how we cook and purchase (like *Green Egg Shopper*) and using up leftovers (*Love Food Hate Waste*) and sharing leftovers (*Foodsharing*, which is currently internet-only).

If you are doing a deep dive in personal care product information, the

*International Nomenclature of Cosmetic Ingredients (INCI)* is the source of info on waxes, oils, pigments, and other chemicals that are used in these products.

If you are looking to increase intake of certain nutrients (like say magnesium), the *World's Healthiest Foods* website (*WHFoods.org*) is brilliant. You can adjust your diet without eating crap you don't like.

## LOCAL FOOD RESOURCES

*Sustainable Agriculture.net* has a blog post with a ton of links to help you find local foods.

But even better? Ask around.

There are plenty of farmers, beekeepers, backyard chicken people, etc in my area that aren't working at that capacity and won't show up on a list, but that I order from because I've found them on social media and/or by asking friends. Then you can go in on a purchase with others in your area which reduces driving/ waste/ and the like.

# UNFUCK YOUR PAIN

The word pain is how we define the discomfort or suffering that we experience as part of illness or injury. It's a general term for a very unique and personal experience. Pain is so intrinsically tied to so many other issues that it ended up being addressed throughout *Unfuck Your Body*, rather than as a separate chapter, but we wanted to make sure some pain management specific tools were included here because this is critical work for so many of us.

And an additional note? If you are having a difficult time having your treatment providers understand how pain is affecting your life, I suggest using and showing them the McGill Pain Scale. It's an excellent and descriptive tool which can support your communication when you are desperate to not just sob and lay on the floor.

## Investigating Your Relationship with Pain

One of the first things we can do is pay attention to our relationship with pain. I know, as someone who has lived with chronic pain for decades, that it gets very easy to just live in it, rather than try to engage with it in new ways. When I've engaged differently, I've seen huge changes in my ability to manage it on a day to day basis, and been able to tolerate

spikes with self-compassion and consideration. While having no pain would be lovely, I don't have that expectation. I just want to be able to continue to live a full and active life, and recognizing that pain is a part of my human experience helps me do that.

Ask yourself the following questions:

How have you put your life on hold because of pain?

Is it the pain or the fight with the pain that is getting in your way?

What are some pain controlling thoughts or strategies you engage in?

What are some pain avoiding thoughts or strategies you engage in?

What are some alternatives that you are willing to try that allow you to honor your pain but still be engaged in your life?

# ACT for Pain

The two big mental components that help with pain are 1) recognizing the influence of thinking patterns on our pain and 2) being mindful of our bodies in the present. Acceptance and Commitment Therapy (ACT) combines both these strategies in a way that has gained a lot of traction in the last decade.

ACT was been described by one of its leading practitioners, Russ Harris, as "a type of therapy that aims to help patients accept what is out of their control, and commit instead to actions that enrichen their lives." I have peppered my previous books with ACT exercises. And there are plenty of people out there incorporating ACT interventions in their lives without going to an ACT therapist by focusing on the six mechanisms for creating more psychological flexibility in your life and seeing how they are influenced by chronic pain.

**Acceptance:** This includes recognizing the thoughts and behaviors that are associated with either trying to control or avoid the pain that are not the healthiest long-term solutions for pain management. I spent years trying to control my pain by ignoring it. Instead of avoiding pain by doing nothing, I pretended it didn't exist at all, constantly overdoing it and making it worse. In my practice I would say this is just as common (if not more common) pain response than trying to control it into submission with medications.

Ways I can accept/respect my pain:

**Cognitive Defusion:** Activities that help disconnect feelings and thoughts that surround our experience of pain from the pain itself, in order to decrease its influence on our lives. (There is an exercise for this in the Mindfulness chapter.)

Ways I can remember that pain is an experience that I am having, but it is not the totality of my existence:

**Being Present:** Mindfulness of your immediate environment rather than being hooked into the pain preoccupations.

Strategies for being present:

**Self as Context:** A perspective about your life in general with pain as only part of it.

What provides meaning in my life?

**Values:** Identifying what matters to you that you want to prioritize above the pain. This helps you recognize how your pain-adaptive behaviors have gotten in the way of your goals.

The values I prioritize:

**Committed Action:** The determination to achieve certain things based on your values while experiencing pain.

How I will show up for myself:

# Pain Log

Tracking your pain probably feels like the least fun thing to do in the world after filing taxes. But as a fellow chronic pain peep, I have learned the hard way that ignoring it makes things way worse. By paying attention I've found multiple ways to stop doing things that make my life harder to manage *and* gotten important information to share with my treatment providers (because the first question out of my LMT's mouth is always "what did you do this time, you stubborn idiot?").

The log below is designed for you to track all your episodes of pain. If you have different pain in two different places on your body at once, create an entry for each one. Sensations regarding different types of pain have been cataloged well with the McGIll Pain Scale, developed by Ronald Melzack in the 1970s and still used today) and these descriptors can be helpful not only for your tracking but to share with your treatment team. Some of the terms you may find helpful include: shooting, stabbing, burning, aching, throbbing, cramping, dull, sharp, numb, tingling, intense, tender, nauseating, hot, exhausting, sore, and any others that suit your specific pain.

Something else I encourage my other pain spoonies to consider? Don't rate the pain based on your personal life with pain if you are trying to get medical help. Your 2 is quite likely a normal person's 8. Consider how a solidly well-off, always had health insurance, reasonably healthy adult who had never experienced this kind of pain in their life would rate this pain if they showed up to the ER saying, "What is *this*????"

| Date/Time | Pain Level (1-10) | Location | Sensations | Weather | Soun[d] sens[ations] |
|---|---|---|---|---|---|
| | | | | | |

| ight rity | Stress level | Energy level | Mental health level | Other symptoms | Medications/ Supplements taken |
|---|---|---|---|---|---|
| | | | | | |

# Headache Log

While I can go about my day in an inordinate amount of pain, add a headache and I'm gonna tap out. Because when you have a headache it can be really hard to think rationally about the headache. So a headache-specific log can be just as (or more important) than a general pain log. When you're thinking about triggers, some areas to look at might be emotional situations, food, hydration, exercise, environmental factors, light, Texas politics, and other life stressors.

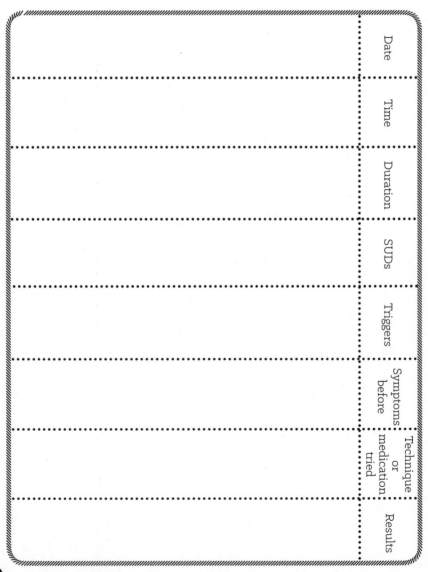

| Date | Time | Duration | SUDs | Triggers | Symptoms before | Technique or medication tried | Results |
|------|------|----------|------|----------|-----------------|-------------------------------|---------|
|      |      |          |      |          |                 |                               |         |
|      |      |          |      |          |                 |                               |         |
|      |      |          |      |          |                 |                               |         |
|      |      |          |      |          |                 |                               |         |
|      |      |          |      |          |                 |                               |         |
|      |      |          |      |          |                 |                               |         |
|      |      |          |      |          |                 |                               |         |

# Humming for Migraines

Tony Bateson, a chronic migraine sufferer, recognized that his migraines dissipated when ranted and raved out loud. So he started studying, first of all, how that could possibly be, and second of all, if he could gain the same effect without the yelly part. He found a good deal of literature on sound healing and came up with the hypothesis that humming at a particular frequency was the part that disrupted the headaches. He began to play with the technique, particularly with mantra meditation, and came up with something that has helped others.

Others have since studied what he came up with and stated that it makes sense. Pain takes control of our brain oscillations (brain waves) and if we use an acoustic that creates an oscillation of the opposite frequencing as the pain oscillation, it would neutralize. Acoustic frequencies, like mantras, have been shown to change the brain. So electrophysiologists think it may help with other pain as well.

The frequency Bateson found most effective to hum is 140 hz, which is essentially a low C sharp. My Buddhist-y and yoga-y readers will recognize this as the same tone as the chanted OM (which is also known as the sound of creation). If you are trying to find that frequency, look for a YouTube video so you don't have to invest in a pitch pipe to get it right. Because I'm super fancy, I have a crystal singing bowl that strikes at 140 hz and I use that in the office for my clients. You can totally do this, but you can't carry it around with you and you can hum anywhere!

You are going to hum with your upper and lower jaw held together, teeth touching, but not a clenched jaw. Try to keep the hum as regular a rhythm as possible.

- Hum for 10 seconds

- Take a deep breath in through the nose

- On the exhale, hum again for 10 seconds

- Repeat for 9 more cycles (ten cycles total of hums)

- Rest for two minutes

- Repeat the sequence (ten cycles and two minutes of rest)

- Then rest for 10 minutes before going about your day

# UNFUCK YOUR MEDICAL TREATMENTS

I know, you've had mixed experiences with medical treatment providers and that whole system. I don't know anyone who hasn't. They save lives and provide treatment, support, and hope. But also sometimes not. There are professionals that are working way out of their depth (this is a nice way of saying unqualified), and there are amazing clinicians hampered by broken systems. Being as proactive as possible about choosing your care providers can help you avoid the latter as much as possible, so let's figure out what that looks like.

## My Treatment Team

This is another one of those "imagine your ideal situation" exercises.

What sort of professionals do you want on your team?

How often do you want to interact with them?

How do you want them to interact with each other?

What are your treatment or diagnosis goals?

# Questions for Treatment Providers

No matter what treatment strategies you are researching, there is a decent chance you are looking for a treatment provider. Whether it is a prescriber, a professional counselor, an occupational therapist to help you find the best weighted blanket, or a nutritionist to help you adjust your diet and add some supplements.

Lifestyle, medical model, or complementary strategies all have experts that may help your journey. But I swear, some days it feels like 99.44% of the battle is finding a provider who you can get in to see in a reasonable amount of time, really listens, is competent in treating you, and is a real partner in helping you get better.

You may be getting treatment in a community mental health setting, where you don't have much choice in providers, but if you do have choices, finding people who you really connect to and can work well with is important. So here are some things to look for when researching plus a place to take notes on what you found:

What is their license and/or certification? Where did they train? Who provides their practice oversight?

List your specific issues and treatment needs: (eg, anxiety, depression, family of origin issues, relationships troubles, etc)

What do they specialize in? What is their treatment approach? What is their training in your specific issues?

What is their experience in treating your personal treatment needs? Are they comfortable with working with your specific issues?

List any other circumstances you have that could impact your care: (eg, medical conditions or disabilities, prejudices you face, your living situation, your financial situation, etc)

Are they comfortable dealing with these issues?

Are they comfortable working with your other providers?

What do they charge? Are there additional fees for other services? How do they accept payment? Do they take insurance? Do they take HSA cards? Will they give you a superbill for reimbursement?

Can they see you soon, and at a time that works with your schedule?

## Questions to Ask Your Prescriber About Medications and Supplements

What symptoms does this medication or supplement treat?

How does it work in the body?

Is this intended for short or long term use?

If it is for short term use what will be our longer term treatment plan?

What side effects could I have from this medication or supplement?

How long will they probably last?

What side effects are dangerous? Which ones mean I should go to an emergency room? Which should I notify you about and how do you want to be notified?

How should I notify you if I want to discuss discontinuing this medication or supplement?

If I no longer want to take this medication will I need to taper off of it?

How long will it take to start working?

Does this medication interact with any other drugs I'm taking?

Does this medication interact with any other supplements or herbs?

What else do you recommend for me to consider in order to help with my symptoms?

## Supplements and Meds

Health professionals love to see a list of everything you're taking (at least they *should*) —and it's helpful to discuss with them what you have tried in the past as well, as you're less likely to have arguments about trying something you already know is incredibly unhelpful.

### CURRENT MEDS AND SUPPLEMENTS

Keep track of everything you regularly take with medicinal intent, including prescriptions, over the counter meds, whole food supplements, synthetic isolate supplements, herbal supplements and teas, homeopathic remedies, therapeutic massages, physical therapy, etc.

| Med/ supplement/ treatment | How often I take this | Dosages | Prescriber | Pharmacy/ store/ website | Brand | Notes/ symptoms |
|---|---|---|---|---|---|---|
| | | | | | | |
| | | | | | | |
| | | | | | | |
| | | | | | | |
| | | | | | | |

## PAST MEDS AND SUPPLEMENTS

Here's where you can keep a running list of things you've tried in the past but stopped taking for whatever reason. Hang onto this when you switch to a new provider so they don't try to put you on the exact same stuff that made you dizzy and angry last time.

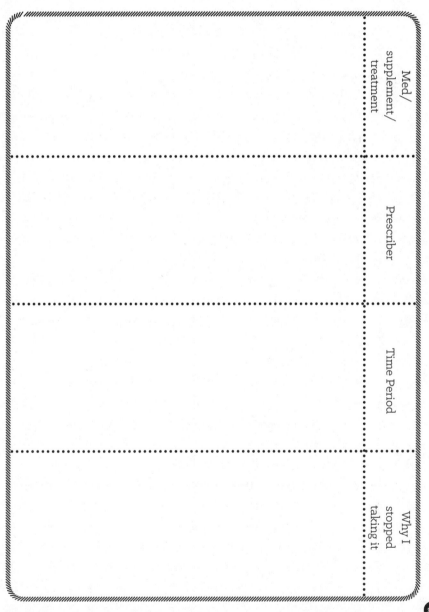

| Med/ supplement/ treatment | Prescriber | Time Period | Why I stopped taking it |
| --- | --- | --- | --- |
|  |  |  |  |
|  |  |  |  |
|  |  |  |  |

# DAILY MEDS AND SUPPLEMENTS TRACKER

Just for you, here's where you can keep track of the pills and potions you take every day!

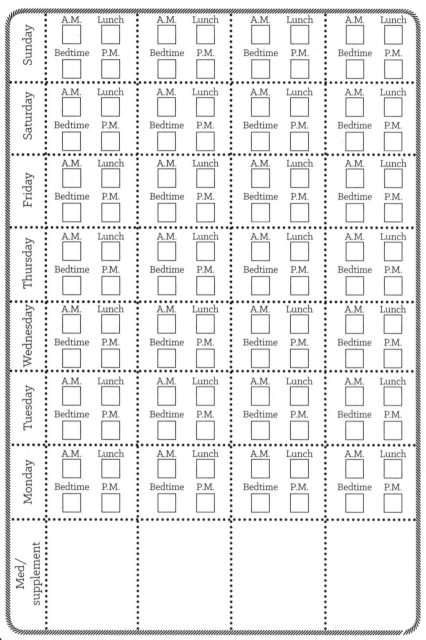

# CRISIS AND SUPPORT LINES

If you're needing extra help at the least opportune time possible (which is the very nature of a crisis, right?), there are a ton of hotlines out there to call, text, email, or chat. Most of them are 24-hour lines, but not all of them, so it's a really good idea to have some backup numbers listed on your crisis plan, just in case. Also, these are all national numbers, so you will likely have different resources in the municipalities in which you live (the United Way 211 line can be a good starting point for finding your local info). They exist for absolutely this reason, and you aren't "taking advantage" of these resources if your regular coping skills aren't helping right now.

## Suicide and Crisis Support Lines

| | |
|---|---|
| Suicide Prevention Hotline | 1-800-SUICIDE (784-2433) |
| Suicide Prevention Hotline En Espanol | 1-888-628-9454 |
| Suicide Prevention Hotline TTY Line (for individuals who are deaf or hard of hearing) | 1-800-799-4889 |
| TeenLine | 1-800-TLC-TEEN |
| The Trevor Hotline (LGBT Crisis Line) | 1-866-4-U-TREVOR |
| Trans Lifeline (Trans or GNC Crisis Line) | 877-565-8860 |
| United Way Helpline | 211 |
| ImAlive | Imalive.org |
| CrisisChat | CrisisChat.org |
| Crisis Text Line | Text HOME to 741741 |
| TeenLine Text | Text "TEEN" to 839863 |

## Abuse and Violence Hotlines

| | |
|---|---|
| National Sexual Assault Telephone Hotline | 800-656-HOPE (4673) |
| National Domestic Violence Hotline | 1-800-799-SAFE |
| National Domestic Violence Hotline En Espanol | 1-800-942-6908 |

| Stop It Now! (Sexual Abuse of Children Hotline) | 1-888-PREVENT |
|---|---|
| Childhelp National Child Abuse Hotline | 1-800-4-A-CHILD (1-800-422-4453) |
| National Center for Missing and Exploited Children | 1-800-THE-LOST |
| National Domestic Violence Hotline | thehotline.org |

## Addictions Support Hotlines

| Marijuana Anonymous | 1-800-766-6779 |
|---|---|
| 24 Hour Cocaine Hotline | 1-800-262-2463 |
| SAMHSA's National Helpline (Treatment Referral Routing Service) | 1-800-662-HELP (4357) |
| National Association for Children of Alcoholics | 1-888-554-2627 |
| National Problem Gambling Helpline Network | 1-800-522-4700 |

## LGBT Support Hotlines

| Lesbian, Gay, Bisexual, and Transgender National Hotline | 1-888-843-4564 |
|---|---|
| Sage LGBT Elder Hotline | 1-888-234-7243 |
| LGBT National Youth Talkline | 1-800-246-PRIDE |
| LGBT National Online Peer Support Chat | glbthotline.org/peer-chat.html |

## Homeless/Runaway Hotlines

| National Runaway/Homeless Hotline | 1-800-231-6946 |
|---|---|
| Boys Town National Hotline | 1-800-448-3000 |
| National Runaway Safeline | 1-800-RUNAWAY (786-2929) |

## Eating Disorder Hotlines

| National Eating Disorders Association Helpline | 1-800-931-2237 |
|---|---|
| National Association of Anorexia Nervosa and Associated Disorders | 1-847-831-3438 |

## Non-Suicidal Self-Injury Hotline

| Self-Injury Hotline | 1-800-DON'T-CUT |
|---|---|

## Poison Control

| Poison Helpline | 1-800-222-1222 |
|---|---|

# About the Author

**Faith G. Harper, PhD, LPC-S, ACS, ACN** is a bad-ass, funny lady with a PhD. She's a licensed professional counselor, board supervisor, certified sexologist, and applied clinical nutritionist with a private practice and consulting business in San Antonio, TX. She has been an adjunct professor and a TEDx presenter, and proudly identifies as a woman of color and uppity intersectional feminist. She is the author of the book *Unf\*ck Your Brain* and many other popular zines and books on subjects such as anxiety, depression, and grief. She is available as a public speaker and for corporate and clinical trainings.